What people are saying about
The Call to Lead...

"Attention all managers – you must read this book to fully understand your role in the workplace. Mr. Harvey has captured the essence of leadership and laid out the tools for easy use."

– Jim Garcia
Manager, Los Angeles Times

"From the Chairman's office to the playing field, one can see how these practical tips are used to enhance leadership qualities... Each chapter maintains a clear and easy-to-understand style that makes this book readable for everyone."

– Cigi Oakley
IBM

"If all leaders subscribe to the tenets presented in *The Call to Lead*, failure becomes obsolete."

– Albert Marino, Ed.D.
Vice President, Diversified Securities, Inc.

"The book offers vital reminders to leaders and subordinates in the industry of what to do and not to do!"

– Souzane Tacawy
Product Manager, Boeing Company

"*The Call to Lead* will assist the manager in fine-tuning the ability to understand others, to listen effectively, communicate clearly and focus on integrity. Humor, candor, and real-life experiences bring these concepts to life. This is a must-read for aspiring managers."

– Ronald D. Stephens
Executive Director, National School Safety Center

The Call to Lead:

How *Ordinary* People Become *Extraordinary* Leaders

By Andrew Harvey

Foreword by
Larry Senn, Ph.D.

Contributing Editor
Amanda Sanders

PUBLISHER'S NOTE

This publication is designed to provide accurate and authoritative information in regard to the subject matter covered. It is sold with the understanding that the publisher is not engaged in rendering legal, psychological, or other professional services. If expert assistance is required, the services of a competent professional person should be sought.

Cypress Publishing Group, Inc.
1835 Roe # 187
Leawood, KS 66211
www.cypresspublishing.com

Library of Congress Cataloging-in-Publication Data

Harvey, Andrew
    The Call to Lead: How Ordinary People Become Extraordinary
Leaders / by Andrew Harvey
    Includes bibliography.
        p.   cm.
    ISBN: 0-89447-326-3
    1.   Leadership in business – United States. 2. Management –
    United States. I. Title.

Printed in the United States of America

January 2002
10 9 8 7 6 5 4 3 2 1

For My Leadership Mentors…
Joseph Molloy
Jeff Templeman
Leon Burrus

Contents

About the Author

Andrew J. Harvey is a captain with a Southern California police agency and has been in law enforcement for more than 20 years. He holds bachelor's and master's degrees from Cal State Los Angeles and is currently a doctoral student at Pepperdine University. He is a graduate of the FBI National Academy and the West Point Leadership Program.

Captain Harvey is an experienced college educator and has been published numerous times in national and international publications. He is a recognized expert in career development and promotional preparation. Through his company, Andrew Harvey Seminars, he provides leadership training and consulting to leaders and organizations throughout the nation.

He can be reached via e-mail at aharvey6@earthlink.net or by mail at:

Andrew Harvey Seminars
PMB #247
2555 Huntington Dr., Suite A
San Marino, CA 91108

ACKNOWLEDGEMENTS

Singer-songwriter Don Henley made an interesting observation about his song, "The Heart of the Matter," a song of great emotional depth. He said it took him four minutes to sing and 40 years to write.

After completing this book, I feel I know what he meant. The first draft of this book was written on a month-long vacation from work, a relatively short time for such an endeavor. However, it has taken me 40 years to be *ready* to write this book.

Although I am listed as the sole author, no one completes such an effort by himself. A great many have helped and supported me, and I would like to offer my thanks to a few of them below.

First and foremost, to Mr. Carl Heintz and the fine people at Cypress Publishing Group, thanks for believing in my work. Thanks also to my editor Amanda Sanders.

Thanks to Dr. Larry Senn of Senn-Delaney Leadership - your foreword added so much. To Keith Bushey, I can't thank you enough for allowing me to use your leadership material. It is some of the best leadership advice I have ever seen. Thank you for allowing me to share your wisdom and experience with others.

Thanks to Chief Bernard Parks and everyone at West Point: Lt. Bill Murphy, Sgt. Bob Medkeff, and Sgt. Gerry Hallanger; to Dr. William Cohen, who provided sage advice and encouragement; to my commuting buddies, Karen Pihlak and Judi Haines, who have provided sympathetic ears and unqualified support to me.

Appreciation to my friend Allen Anderson, who really doesn't have a mean bone in his body. Thanks for the 98 in '85. It set the wheels in motion. Gratitude to Jim Hope for being a great dad under difficult circumstances; to my friend Tom Hunter, thanks for watching over me when I was just a pup. To my friend

Elliot Kase, it has been quite a ride since Jan. 2, 1981. I've enjoyed it and can safely say it would not have been the same without you.

Thanks to Chief Dennis Kies, a great friend. Your support has meant so much to me, particularly during the tough times. To John Lentz, I would like to say thanks for taking a chance on me when it would have been very easy not to. Although there have been times I've regretted your decision, I hope you never have. Much gratitude to Dr. Al Marino, you are much more than a great advisor, you are a great friend; to all my Pepperdine buddies, but especially Cigi Oakley and Souzane Tacawy, thanks for everything. To Darryl Mounger, thanks for being a part of my team and for being so fair with me. Without your efforts, I may not have been in a position to write this book.

To Don Lacher, my friend and fellow instructor, you're a great guy, and I appreciate your friendship; thanks to Daryl Gates for the support and encouragement over the years. To Shirley Von, what can I say? If people thought of me as you do, I would be the King of the World. Thanks for everything. To my friends at Covina Sunrise Rotary, thanks for all you do. A portion from the proceeds of this book will go to Operation Santa Clothes.

To my oldest friend, Brent Weber, we're a long way from Tucker. It's been great having you as a friend. To Larry Waldie, thanks for your friendship and support; to Bob Browne, thanks for showing me what a consummate professional looks like; to Layfayette Parish, my one and only brother, thanks for the good times; to Jim and Gina Garcia, you guys are the best - thanks for everything.

To Dr. Vance Caesar, thanks for all your sage advice and encouragement. I can see why you're the best executive coach in the business. My thanks to a true gentleman, Dr. Ron Stephens. Your suggestions and support have proven invaluable. To Al Lewis and the Lewis family, thanks for the support over the years.

Lastly and mostly, my love and thanks to my heaven-sent angels. Thank you for every minute of every day.

Foreword

Countless books have been written to try to explain the art and science of leadership. *The Call to Lead* is different. It is straightforward, common sense, easy to read, and immediately useful. For new leaders or those aspiring to lead, the book provides a strong foundation for most all aspects of leadership. For experienced managers, it provides a great checklist for "how I'm doing." It will help you to inventory your current skills and create a to-do list of what you need to work on. That's important because never before in history has leadership effectiveness been so important to organizations or to managers at all levels. Understanding how to manage may be adequate when an organization is in a steady state; leadership skills are vital when facing change. And who isn't facing change?

Even though I have been involved in teaching leadership for 30 years at universities, through a leadership-consulting firm I founded, and in books I've written, I found *The Call to Lead* to be valuable and enjoyable.

The author weaves in interesting quotes, extensive real-life experience, anecdotes from authorities in the field, and humorous stories to illustrate his common-sense approach to leadership. I also found the format of bite-sized chapters, each covering one aspect of leadership, easy to digest. Topics include teamwork, communications, decision making, and change. Each chapter contains suggestions on objective things to do and each displays a sensitivity toward people.

I have always believed that becoming a leader is a journey, not a destination. *The Call to Lead* provides another step in that journey by covering the foundational essence of good leadership and by helping to prepare a leader to face most any leadership situation that may arise.

Larry Senn

Dr. Larry Senn is Chairman of Senn-Delaney Leadership, an international leadership-consulting firm which is a part of Provant. He is co-author of *21st Century Leadership*, *Leaders on Leading,* and *Secrets of a Winning Culture.*

Introduction

This book was written as an antidote to the *Dilbert* comic strip. Don't get me wrong; I love the strip and have cut it out of the paper on many occasions. Scott Adams' delicious skewering of management and the corporate environment is true to life. The utter insanity portrayed in the strip actually goes on in many workplaces.

I have heard from several people on occasions about incidents in the strip that actually happened in their workplace. I have also seen quite a few with my own eyes. It's as if Mr. Adams has his spies everywhere. It is sad to me that the workplace has become such a parody. Is managerial incompetence at an all-time high? Has there been such a decline in the quality of leadership that there is no hope of recovery?

I don't think so, but I do believe there is a long road to improvement ahead. *The Call to Lead: How Ordinary People Become Extraordinary Leaders* was written to help leaders restore and bolster some of the respect and faith workers once had in them.

I have worked in law enforcement for 20 years, spending the last 15 years at the supervisory, management, and executive levels. My field is a unique one, quasi-military but community based. I have seen people at their worst and have had occasion to lead under the most adverse of conditions.

Over the last 20 years, I have been both a student and practitioner of leadership, and I've taken a lot of notes along the way. This book represents those experiences. I have worked with leaders who were brilliant, and I have worked with leaders who were incompetent. Broken down to its most basic form, leadership is simply dealing with people. This is true regardless of the venue. *The Call to Lead* has its foundation in a law enforcement approach to leadership because that has been my proving ground. However, the lessons learned can be put to use in almost any leadership arena.

The Call to Lead takes the position that there are three critical components of good leadership: common sense, logic, and concern for people. These form in essence a "leadership triangle." Although each of the three components is important, how they work together is equally as important. As you'll notice in reading this book, some issues overlap into one or both of the other components. Good leaders blend the characteristics of each of the components into their everyday behavior.

As human beings, it is natural that we may not be equally as adept at each portion of this triangle. The purpose of this book is to first help leaders recognize these three necessary components. Once this is accomplished, leaders should do a perpetual self-inventory on the characteristics of each component, always attempting to bring together all three areas when approaching leadership opportunities.

I do not believe that as a general rule buffoons are placed into management positions. Most people who are promoted into a management position have a workable amount of common sense, logic, and concern for people. The real test is how people respond when placed into such positions. Everyone changes when they are promoted; it is just a question of degree. Unfortunately, for some, a promotion means their ability to excel in managerial areas seems to drain out of their feet, and we are left with the pointy-haired boss from *Dilbert*.

Further, I don't believe that common sense, logic, or concern for people can be taught to those who have no such aptitude. What I do believe is that leaders who have lost their way can be redeemed. This book is an effort to assist them in recognizing problem areas and ways for correction. The book is also written for those aspiring to leadership positions, because it is better to put these concepts to work from day one.

Leadership is not rocket science. It is a very straightforward combination of science and art. Leadership is the ability to get things done through others. When work products and results can be produced in a positive and supportive environment, effective leadership has occurred. Leadership is about demonstrating your courage, character, commitment, and competence.

People are desperate for good leadership. Let's give them what they want.

4 The Call to Lead

Before You Begin

No one can be a good leader without self-knowledge. Usually, a leader is thought of as looking outward and evaluating external conditions, but good leadership must begin with a base of self-knowledge, and this begins with looking inward. Before you can be effective at leading others, you must know yourself.

At some point, in every leader's foundation, there must come recognition of who you are and who you are not. This includes your strengths and weaknesses. Meditation and reflection may be used as a way to help examine yourself. Who are you? What do you value?

After you have answered these questions, you can create your own personal vision. This is different from the vision statement that you create for your organization. A personal vision helps you to examine whether or not your life is congruent with your basic values and beliefs. Do you act in accordance with your values? Is your life following the direction you set out for it? Are you using means to accomplish your goals that are in line with your vision? Harmony comes from accomplishing your dreams but doing so in a manner consistent with your ethics. Viktor Frankl said, "We all have some vision of ourselves and our future. And that vision creates consequences more than any other factor; vision affects the choices we make and the way we spend our time."

You should examine this vision to see if it is shallow or deep. Is it "me-centered" and selfish? Or is it centered on ideas of helping and doing something good in the world? Leaders who focus solely on selfish, shallow goals – making more money, being able to afford an expensive car, obtaining more power – may not be as fulfilled and successful as they appear. Good, enduring leaders do not focus solely on themselves. Instead, these leaders are driven by great causes about which they feel passionate.

This great cause does not necessarily have to be a heroic effort. It is, however, something above self and beyond the everyday, and it is in line with your own moral and spiritual self. Those who focus on a vision that is outwardly directed, spiritually aligned, and noble in its cause have a sense of enthusiasm and fulfillment.

Your vision does not have to be grandiose, but it should be larger than yourself. It may only affect a handful of people, but that does not mean that it is not valuable and needed. What is important is that you are using all of your talents to their greatest degree. As in Jesus' "Parable of the Talents," you lose out when you do not develop and use your talents and skills.

You may want to begin with the personality evaluation on the CD ROM available with this book. This is a good starting point to assess your personality and your leadership style. From there, you can determine what areas you need to develop, what your strengths are, and how to compliment them. Then, you can study the concepts in this book from a more personal vantage point.

On the CD ROM, you will also find "Be a Leader," an article by Keith D. Bushey, which provides helpful tips that can guide you as you strive to become a better leader. There is also a lot of free software to help you better manage your time, resources, and employees. All of these tools are designed to help you be a more effective leader.

As a leader, you are being called upon to use your talents to their greatest degree and eventually to help others do the same. First, you must know yourself. This book will help you in the self-evaluation process. It will also help you to develop skills so that you can help others. In doing so, you will answer the call to lead.

8 The Call to Lead

Common Sense

Common sense is uncommon in life. It is a difficult concept to describe, but people recognize when it is being applied. They also recognize when it is not being employed. Common sense plays a great role in leadership. Obstacles that occur on a daily basis must be dealt with, and only common sense can penetrate the complexity of many problems.

Most leaders possess common sense; they just may not display it as often as they should in their leadership approach. This section addresses eighteen key leadership areas that can be impacted with a common sense approach. This component is not free-standing and should be accompanied by the two other essential elements of leadership, logical analysis and concern for people.

10 The Call to Lead

The Goal of Leadership

Leadership involves remembering past mistakes, an analysis of today's achievements, and a well-grounded imagination in visualizing the problems of the future.

–Stanley Allyn

Leaders are facing a daunting challenge in the new millenium. As Robert Tannenbaum and Warren H. Schmidt said:

> [Societal changes] make effective leadership in the future a more challenging task, requiring even greater sensitivity and flexibility than was ever needed before. Today's manager is more likely to deal with employees who resent being treated as subordinates, who may be highly critical of any organizational system, who expect to be consulted and to exert influence, and who often stand on the edge of alienation from the institution that needs their loyalty and commitment. In addition, he is frequently confronted by a highly turbulent, unpredictable environment.
>
> (from the article, "How to Choose a Leadership Pattern," featured in the *Harvard Business Review*)

Most experienced leaders immediately identify with this statement. However, if you think that these are only recent problems, you would be wrong. This article was written almost 30 years ago, in 1973.

Have leaders risen to today's challenges? Not necessarily, if you rely upon these sample evaluations of officers reputedly taken from the files of the British Royal Navy.

- His men would follow him anywhere but only out of curiosity.

- This officer reminds me of a gyroscope — always spinning at a frantic pace but not really going anywhere.

- Since my last report, he has reached rock bottom and started to dig.

- He sets low standards and then consistently fails to achieve them.

- This pilot should not be allowed to fly below 250 feet.

- Works well when under constant supervision and cornered like a rat in a trap.

- This man is depriving a village somewhere of an idiot.

These extreme examples of military officers showcase leaders who do not know how to lead, but it is difficult to become a good leader without first having mastered the art of following. Good leaders are invariably good followers first. Leading requires sensitivity to the follower's position and the knowledge, based on experience, of what motivates a person to follow a good leader.

President Dwight Eisenhower demonstrated the art of leadership with a simple piece of string. He would put it on a table and say, "pull it, and it'll follow wherever you wish; *push* it, and it will go nowhere at all." This is a telling illustration of the balance required by good leaders.

Through experience, a leader learns which tactics are successful and which are not. Using pure positional authority, you can get people to do things to a certain point. There are methods, such as fear or negative reinforcement, which make this style of motivation work. A good leader may use any of these tactics, depending on the situation and the people involved. However, if this is the only way that you can gain compliance, you will likely never reach the top mantle of leadership.

Through such techniques, often called "Theory X," you may be able to control people's bodies and even their minds to some degree. To win their hearts, you must go much further. You must be willing to coach, mentor, support, and gently guide people toward the path you want them to follow. It is indeed the art of demonstrating to people that it is in their best interests to follow you.

The goal of leadership is to get people to work *willingly* toward accomplishing the goals of the organization. No amount of authority, coercion, or fear will make this occur. It is only through the pulling of Eisenhower's string that people will follow with their best effort.

Chapter Analysis

Keys to Understanding

- Being a good leader requires having been a good follower.

- Focus on getting people to *willingly* work toward organizational goals.

Questions for Reflection

1. Can you remember instances when you demonstrated that you were a good follower? What were they?

2. Think back to when you were a follower. What was your leader like? Did that person do anything that made you want to follow or not follow?

3. What is the difference between "pushing" an employee and "pulling" one?

14 The Call to Lead

Vision

If you don't know where you're going, any road will get you there.

–Cheshire Cat in *Alice's Adventures
in Wonderland*

*The very essence of leadership is that you have to have a vision. It's got to
be a vision you can articulate clearly and forcefully on every occasion. You
can't blow an uncertain trumpet.*

–Father Theodore Hesburgh, University of
Notre Dame

The first and foremost responsibility of leaders is to
have a vision of where they want to take their organizations.
This is not something one can find in a book, be it this one or
any other. It must emanate naturally from the heart and
mind. Although it is fine to seek out as much information
about the organization as possible, the leader must intrin-
sically have a firm sense of direction. If the leader does not
possess this vision, the organization will quickly become a head-
less horse, galloping in all different directions but not really
getting anywhere.

If leaders cannot create a compelling vision for the
organization, their leadership is seriously impaired. Your
vision does not have to be too grand or lofty, but you must be
clear, at least in your own mind, of where you perceive the
destiny of the corporation to lie. Your vision should be
meaningful and concrete, so that it is easy for people to rally

behind it. It must also be credible, in the sense that people believe it is possible to achieve.

A vision statement expresses the aspirations of the organization. It identifies the direction of the organization, what it hopes to become, and the principles it will follow to achieve its goals. It should encompass the core beliefs and values of the organization.

Within the vision, you create a type of guide as to how your organization will conduct itself: how customers will be served, how employees will be treated, how the organization will serve its social or environmental responsibilities, and how the company will be structured. The vision reflects the reason for the formation of the organization and possibly even the industry. For example, the law enforcement sector was established to preserve an orderly society, and this idea would certainly be incorporated into my vision for a unit.

Formulating a corporate vision requires an assessment of the organization's history and culture; the expectations of the stockholders, employees, customers and suppliers; and an appreciation of the place the organization occupies in the larger society. These factors, plus the societal imperatives, should guide the formulation of a corporate vision. Increasingly, leaders are incorporating faith-based concepts into their vision. Issues of corporate responsibilities to preserve and protect the environment, enhance the communities they occupy, fulfill social responsibilities to the disadvantaged, and provide a family-oriented work environment reflect the increasingly important aspects of social accountability.

The vision serves to unify the organization with a shared purpose. This communal goal gives a sense of commitment and focus to every member of an organization and motivates them to fulfill the aspirations of the vision. A purposeful direction also gives individuals confidence because they know where they are headed. A strong vision statement can be used for planning and problem solving by both employees and leaders. It lets every member know what the priorities of the organization are and what principles are guiding all decisions. When conflicts arise, the vision state-ment can be looked upon as a reference point, a map that shows the destination of the company and the means it employs in order to reach that goal.

A wise leader incorporates multiple aspects into the vision. It becomes a guiding force to incorporate societal concerns, the well-being of employees, and sustainable growth in a long-term plan. Often, leaders spend weeks wrestling with the sometimes-contradictory demands of various corporate and societal imperatives. In the end, the leader must make the choice that results in compromise. Intense meditation often facilitates this arduous process. A focus group of key employees, officers, directors, and advisors is often used as a sounding board for the evolving vision.

At some point, the formulation phase must transition into the adoption phase. The leader must become the foremost advocate of the vision; it must be definite, defined, and delin-eated. The mind and soul of the leader must be fully committed, and it becomes his or her "mantra" to the organization.

> **Leadership begins when the executive can "own" the corporate vision, articulate it clearly, and passionately advocate for it.**

A leader must personally "own" the vision before at-tempting to incorporate it into the organization. The leader must also be passionate about this vision for it is not likely that it will sustain itself. Without a vision, an organization may become directionless and end up following the personal whims and quirks of the leader.

Many people have worked for bosses who did not have clear visions for the organization. As a result, the employees end up trying to please the boss on a day-to-day basis without an idea for the larger goals or long-term directions of the company. This creates a "fire department" group where the most important thing is the current task. Workers are not directing their actions to serve a long-term goal or higher purpose. If a leader cannot effectively articulate a compelling vision, the result is the same as not having one at all. Being able to effectively communicate ideas is as important as having them.

Once you have a clear vision, the hard part begins: communicating it to the organization so that everyone understands it. Once, I worked for a boss who claimed to have a great organizational vision. I believed him even though I had no tangible proof. I assumed that he had it clear in his own mind, until later when it became evident that he did not really possess the vision I had thought he had. He did his best to fake it, but his effort was ultimately futile. People will follow such a leader for a while until they realize the real lack of vision, at which point disillusionment sets in.

In their superb book, *The Leadership Challenge*, Jim Kouzes and Barry Posner address the importance of the leader's sharing a vision with the organization:

> Leadership vision is necessary but insufficient for an organization to move forward with purpose toward a common destination. As important, if not more so, is the ability to communicate that vision so that others come to see what the leader sees. Followers, in fact, have no idea what a leader's vision is until the leader describes it.

The vision needs to be effectively communicated to the organization in a variety of ways and repeated frequently. A simple memo of what the vision is may be a good start, but it doesn't end there. Personal communication of the vision by the leader is mandatory, both in groups and individually. Examples should be used to provide further illustration. Metaphors, analogies, models, or even humor can all be used to make the vision understandable. Part of the responsibility of management is to constantly be aware of the vision; leaders must restate, refresh, remind, and repeat the vision often.

Repeating the vision so many times should not be boring for the leader who truly believes the message. At this point, remember that there will still be people in the organization who have not heard the message, have forgotten it, or don't understand how it applies to them. You must be passionate in your communication of the vision. Just when you can hardly stand to say it again, there will be someone in the organization who is just hearing it for the first time. Just like a good teacher, leaders tell and retell their lesson; they emphasize and restate, convince and illuminate everyone in the organization.

Once you feel you have effectively articulated your vision, then missions, values, goals, and objectives must be identified and communicated in order to support the vision. This is hard work, but it produces results and will serve as the organization's emotional foundation for further work efforts.

In *The Secret of a Winning Culture,* Larry E. Senn and John Childress make an astute observation about vision. They state, "A compelling vision consists of two elements: a future-state that captures our imagination and a passionate desire to reach it."

This point is illustrated in a story about Walt Disney's approach to building Disneyland. His highly competent planners and engineers had laid out a precise plan for what would be built and in what order. There was a logical progression, so that one area's completion would flow naturally into the next. Within this plan, the centerpiece castle was to be built last.

Walt Disney changed this plan and had the castle built first, over the objection of his staff. His reason can be found in

his vision. He wanted the castle to be built first so that everyone working on the remainder of the project would be able to
see it. In his view, the castle was the tangible example of the
magic kingdom he had in mind; it was the bricks-and-mortar
realization of his vision. What a great example of communicating one's vision in a most unique way.

In his book, *Managing People is like Herding Cats,* Warren
Bennis takes note of the importance of vision and the necessary follow-up once the vision is identified:

> Executives must not just articulate a simple and
> compelling vision, but they must take this vision into
> account when doing everything that they do – when
> thinking about recruiting and reward systems, when
> considering empowerment, when changing the
> structure, when pursuing new markets, and when
> making decisions.
>
> The only way a leader is going to translate vision
> into reality – an ability that is the essence of leader-
> ship – is to anchor policies, practices, procedures, and
> systems that will bring in people and empower them
> to implement the vision.

Developing a persuasive vision, articulating it per-
petually, and incorporating it into the organizational culture
are not easy tasks. However, if accomplished correctly, each
person will know what needs to be done. Most of those who
are working in contradiction to the vision will stand out.
Then these individuals can be coached and counseled to work
toward the vision. If this is ineffective, other measures may
become necessary, including firing those who are impediments
to the realization of the vision.

In discussions of great leaders, Abraham Lincoln's
name invariably comes up. Leaders would do well to emulate
his approach to creating and communicating a vision.

Abraham Lincoln's approach to vision is interpreted in
Donald T. Phillips' book, *Lincoln on Leadership*:

- Provide a clear, concise statement of the direction of your
  organization and justify the actions you take.

- Everywhere you go, at every conceivable opportunity,
  reaffirm, reassert, and remind everyone of the basic
  principles upon which your organization was founded.

- Effective visions can't be forced on the masses. Rather, you
  must set them in motion by means of persuasion.

- Harness your vision through implementation of your own
  personal leadership style.

- When you preach your vision, don't shoot too high. Aim
  lower, and the common people will understand you. They
  are the ones you want to reach – at least they are the ones
  you ought to reach.

Vision Checklist

It is imperative that a leader has a strong vision in order to
successfully guide an organization. Here is a list of the most
essential elements of a fully developed corporate vision:

✓ It can be expressed in simple terms.

✓ Everyone in the organization can understand it.

✓ It is concrete, and its achievement can be measured.

✓ It is credible and feasible.

✓ It is consistent with the history, culture, and expectations
  of the organization.

✓ It considers the "bigger picture" or how the organization
  fits into society.

Chapter Analysis

Keys to Understanding

- As a top leader, you must have an overall vision for your organization.

- You must also be able to articulate the vision in terms that are understandable to everyone.

- The vision must be credible so that people can believe in it and feel that it is achievable.

- Communicate the vision constantly and ensure that it pervades the tiniest corners of the organization.

- Ensure that the vision is not contradicted in any organizational policy, practice, procedure, or action.

Questions for Reflection

1. What is the overall vision of your organization? How does it differ from your "mission statement?"

2. In what way is your personal vision different from the organization's?

3. Are there contradictions between your personal vision and the organization's?

4. What steps have you taken to articulate your vision and communicate it?

Chapter 3

Clear Direction

If we don't change our direction, we're likely to end up where we're headed.

–Chinese proverb

Not providing clear direction is one of the most common mistakes a leader can make. Employees want to know what is expected of them and when the task in question must be completed. They also want to know any restrictions or parameters up front, so they do not go in the wrong direction and waste valuable time.

Many employees have shared stories with me in which they finished a long-term project, only to be told by their boss, "Well, that's not exactly what I was looking for." The boss did not bother to clearly articulate what was wanted, so the employees were left without guidelines.

Another version of this is the boss who fails to keep people informed. I was once given a major project to complete. The project involved statistical research and developing a variety of charts and graphs. After working on the project for several weeks, I turned it in to my boss. Without the least hint of remorse or regret, he advised me that the direction had changed, and the project was no longer needed. I remember thinking to myself that I would have to include this in the leadership book I would write one day. Not communicating that changes in projects or policies have occurred wastes time. Far worse, it demonstrates a lack of respect for your employees.

Leaders should be as clear as possible about what is desired from an employee when a task is assigned. If a leader is not clear on the goals of a project, it should not be assigned. It is unproductive and disrespectful to have employees making frantic efforts to please you, when you, the leader, don't even know what you want. The "I'll know it when I see it" philosophy just doesn't work. This is not a window-shopping excursion where you can browse around until something catches your eye. Sometimes it seems that the delegation of projects is an effort to keep people busy. This is a symptom of a larger problem of human-resource planning and an example of "fire engine" management. Leaders have a responsibility to not waste people's time or corporate resources.

Once the task is clear in your mind, you should identify when you need the project accomplished. Don't set meaningless or false deadlines. Give your employee a fair and realistic goal for completion. Once you receive the project, don't let it sit on your desk for six months. I've heard countless complaints from people about such actions. It usually sounds like this: "I busted my butt to get this thing done on time and then it sits on his desk for six months with no action! That's the last time I'm going to do that." One of the greatest ways to show respect for people is to respect their time. If you impose a deadline, make sure you do your part when the employee meets that deadline. Let the person know in the beginning if there are restrictions on how the task is to be accomplished. This saves time and gives people additional confidence in the job they are performing.

A leader must be clear on how the goals of an organization are to be accomplished. I have worked for two bosses who I believe were intentionally unclear in their direction. The first one had honorable motives, and the second one did not. In the first situation, the boss would not give clear direction as a way of mentoring people. He figured the less direction he gave, the more people would have to fend for themselves and figure it out on their own. He felt this would help them develop more quickly than if he gave them precise instructions.

This "sink-or-swim" approach has its merits but also its limitations. I believe the boss should have made it very clear *what* he wanted accomplished. This would have created an unambiguous, definite goal for the employee. *How* the job was going to be accomplished within the stated parameters could have been left to the employee. People have their own style of working and should be free to follow it. This approach would have created clear direction while still allowing people to figure out the process they would use on their own. Some people like to have explicit instructions and follow a plan. His approach made it difficult to do that.

The other ambiguous boss had more devious motives. His directions never clarified what was to be accomplished. Goals were always stated in uncertain terms. Even when aggressively pressed, the boss would not come forward with more precise instructions, and this was frustrating to his employees. We could not understand why a boss would not want to give clear direction.

We soon noticed that when a project was successful, the boss would take the credit, making sure to inform his boss of the success. On the other hand, when a project failed, the boss would claim that we had not carried out his orders properly. If reminded exactly what his directions were, he would deny ever having given such orders. Of course, he would inform his boss that his instructions had not been properly followed. This left his reputation with his superior somewhat intact, as successes were attributable to his efforts, and failures were blamed on incompetent subordinates who could not properly follow orders. Although he was able to temporarily gain favor with his boss, he lost all the respect and support of his people. This type of loss can be survived for a transitory period of time but eventually the troops rebel.

Leaders must have the conviction to give clear direction to their people and stand behind them regardless of resultant success or failure.

Chapter Analysis

Keys to Understanding

- Make no assignment until it is clear in your own mind what you want.

- Tell people *what* is desired but, to the degree possible, give them the freedom to figure out *how* to accomplish the task.

- If there are parameters, state them up front.

- If there is a change in your direction, notify people immediately. If possible, explain the reasoning behind the change.

Questions For Reflection

1. How do you ensure that your people are informed about what is expected of them?

2. Are you entirely certain how the goals of your organization are to be accomplished?

3. How do you deal with the conflict between advancing your career and helping your subordinates gain recognition?

Chapter 4

Action vs. Words

What you do speaks so loudly that I cannot hear what you say.

–Ralph Waldo Emerson

Example is leadership.

–Dr. Albert Schweitzer

The difference between actions and words is highlighted in the role of leader. People will no doubt listen to what you have to say if you are in a position of leadership. Over time, they will compare what you say to what you do. If there is a disparity, your credibility will diminish. This could be disastrous as credibility is critical to effective leadership.

In *The Leadership Challenge*, Kouzes and Posner state:

We know that leaders' deeds are far more important than their words. Credibility of action is the single most significant determinant of whether a leader will be followed over time.

It is confusing to workers when their boss gives them good advice while setting a bad example. People may doubt what you say, but they will almost always believe what you do. If the two are not complementary, your employees will see this. People lose respect for leaders who do not match actions and words. They may also lose their willingness to follow.

You can only lead others where you yourself are willing to go. You must state the way *and* show the way. Recounted below is an illustrative story about General George Patton:

In 1942, General Patton took command of the Desert Training Center. Upon his arrival, all officers and enlisted men stood for inspection. Patton advised them that everyone under his command would be required to run a mile in fifteen minutes carrying their rifle and full military pack. He said, "We will start running from this point in exactly thirty minutes. I will lead."

It is not a common sight in the military to see a general running a mile with a rifle and full military pack on his back. That, however, is exactly what General Patton did. His actions provided a very tangible demonstration of leading by example. Patton, for whatever faults he may have had, always ensured that his actions mirrored his words.

As a law enforcement officer, I felt the importance of matching my own actions to what I expected from others. Driving a patrol car, I was a very visible representative of the traffic laws I sought to enforce. Except when driving in emergency mode, if I had been seen not signaling, speeding, or following too closely, I would not have been an effective agent of the law. For when I pulled over another for committing the same offenses, I would have lost credibility in that person's eyes. Actions become the determinant of your credibility.

Chapter Analysis

Keys to Understanding

- In almost all cases, people will believe your actions above your words.

- Credibility of action is the biggest determinant of whether you as a leader will be followed over time.

- Make every effort to lead by example.

Questions for Reflection

1. How credible a leader are you perceived to be?

2. Which of these "little indiscretions" do you take advantage of at work:

   a. Personal calls

   b. Use of copy machine for personal use

   c. Taking time to do personal errands

   d. Use of the Internet

   e. Taking home office supplies

3. How do you communicate your integrity?

The Use of Power

Power intoxicates men. When a man is intoxicated by alcohol he can recover, but when intoxicated by power, he seldom recovers.

–James Byrnes

Nearly all men can stand adversity, but if you want to test a man's character, give him power.

–Abraham Lincoln

In my role as a command-level law enforcement officer, people have often asked me about the best part of my job. Without hesitation, I always answer "power." People are often shocked by that response, thinking I have perhaps become "power mad." I then explain that power can be used either positively or negatively. I always try my best to use my power for good purposes. When power is backed with a conscience, it can have a very beneficial impact on the organization.

Although power can be used to impact major issues in an organization, it can also be used for the little things. Seemingly minor gestures often leave lasting and meaningful impressions. You may often have the opportunity to use your authority in positive ways to help employees do their jobs more productively. This type of support is easily recognized and valued.

For example, one day as I was walking through my organization's records section, one of the clerks mentioned that they needed an industrial-size three-hole punch for the large reams of paper they must process. The one they had been using for many years was in a state of disrepair. Requests had been made for a new one, but somehow these requests had been lost in the bureaucracy. I left and drove to the local office supply store where I purchased a new punch. When I walked into Records and presented them with it, they were stunned but very happy.

I took the above action for two reasons. On a practical level, they really needed the new hole punch to properly perform their work. More personally, by handling their request myself, they knew that top management really did care about them. In the long run, this meant much more than just acquiring a new hole punch for the staff. It was probably the most productive action I took all day because it had an immediate effect. I used my authority in a positive manner by purchasing the punch and made a significant impact on the attitudes of my staff.

Kouzes and Posner stated their position on the use of power in eloquent terms in *The Leadership Challenge*:

> Managers who focus on themselves and are insensitive to others fail. They fail because there is a limit to what they can do by themselves. Leaders succeed when they realize that the limits to what can be accomplished are minimal if people feel strong and capable. In fact, what leaders do, as paradoxical as it may seem, is make followers into leaders. They do this by using their own power in service of others rather than in service of self.

There are different types of power a leader may possess. There is a certain amount of power that comes with the position. There are also other forms of power based upon certain expertise, personal connections, and even natural charisma. The irony is that the higher up you go in an organization, the more dependent you become on others.

Along with any type of power comes responsibility. The use of power is one of the biggest responsibilities of a leader. Most everyone has worked for a boss who abused power. The use of power by a leader often demonstrates the morals, ethics, and principles of the organization. Far too often, power is seen to be a "perk" to provide extravagant benefits on behalf of those holding it. Sometimes, it is used to consolidate influence and stop opposition within the company. When power is abused in these ways, it can affect the integrity of the leader and the organization as a whole.

Excessive exercise of power occasionally causes an entire organization to crumble. When Leona Hensley was at her peak of power, her hotels were used to provide extravagant benefits to her and her family. Eventually, the exercise of power led to an arrogance and disregard for tax laws, setting the stage for the eventual demise of the organization.

Thus, a leader must be aware of the intoxicating effects power can have. We have all seen those whose inability to deal with power led to abuses of discretion. Power can blind some people and lead to errors in judgment. Good leaders are certainly not afraid to use their power, but they use it to make a positive difference in their organization.

Chapter Analysis

Keys to Understanding

- As a leader, use your power regularly to help people do their jobs.

- Remember that power can be either a positive or negative force. A good leader uses power positively as much as possible.

Questions for Reflection

1. In what ways have you used your power and authority to improve the conditions of your subordinates?

2. Why is power too intoxicating? Do leaders know when power has "gone to their heads?"

3. Do you like power? If so, why?

Chapter 6

Teamwork

No matter how much work a man can do, no matter how engaging his personality may be, he will not advance far in business if he cannot work with others.

–John Craig

Everyone probably knows at least one "individualist" who is a nonconformist and cannot fit into a group or function as part of a team. Successful entrepreneurs are often portrayed as members of this class of rebels, along with writers and artists, who shun traditional organizational structures to "do their own thing."

The facts are quite different from the perceptions. While you could find poor team players in any field or in any organization, entrepreneurs or small business owners must have exceptional team skills to recruit and retain the right people.

The concept of "team player" is often used without an adequate definition. What is the basic tenant of "team" action in business? Some purists would say that in a team, the individual's self-interest is subjugated to the team's objectives. Others would argue that "being a team player" merely implies a loyalty to the company and dedication to the job.

In much of American business, work has been broken into projects, which are then assigned to corporate teams. This "project-oriented" workflow has become

increasingly popular. Then there are those who would
argue that "team" concepts have been too enthusiastically
applied in business. When Japanese teamwork constructs
were introduced in U.S. businesses, some American workers
chafed under the burden of the teamwork environment.
They were not always so willing to put the interests of a
team above that of their own careers.

One cannot dismiss the individualist as a heretic just
because they do not work well in a "cooperative team" of
four or five people. Especially in a small business, "team
players" may not be the perfect employees. In situations
requiring unique solutions or intense creative work, other
workplace personalities may be more effective.

Small businesses often function as one team. There
is little distinction between members of the executive group
and workers. This works well in many situations. On the
other hand, the older chain-of-command approach may be
more appropriate in a larger business.

Whether your organization is a full team-oriented organization, a traditional chain of command, or a hybrid,
the full commitment to the organization by each participant
is critical. If a leader is to expect high-quality production,
this must be communicated and modeled by the leader's
own behavior. This means there will be times when leaders
could impose their wills if they so desired but choose not to
for the betterment of the group. When leaders do this,
people notice. It is even more apparent when they fail to
keep the group's goal as the top priority.

Good teamwork creates a synergistic effect where
combined efforts are much greater than the sum of the individual parts. One of a leader's most important duties is to
create an environment where teamwork can thrive.
Teamwork often produces greater results than individual
efforts. In essence, teamwork divides the effort and
multiplies the effect.

The importance of teamwork is illustrated in the following anecdote:

> At a county fair, the townspeople held a horse-pulling contest. The first-place horse ended up moving a sled weighing 4,500 pounds. The second-place finisher pulled 4,000 pounds. The owners of the two horses decided to see what these horses could pull together. They hitched them up and found that the team could move 12,000 pounds. By working separately, the two horses were good for only 8,500 pounds. When coupled together, their joint effort produced an added 3,500 pounds.

Good leaders reward workers for their efforts and focus on those who are not being team players. Initially, coaching and counseling can be effective in getting a person to work within the team concept. If this is ineffective, the non-team player may have to be dealt with more harshly. Ultimately, if people are working to the detriment of the organization, and their attitudes cannot be reformed, termination of employment is probably the best choice.

Many will be watching to see how the leader handles the situation. If team players are rewarded, and non-team players are dealt with effectively, this will send a strong message about the importance of teamwork. A leader sends such a message on a continual basis.

The Senn-Delaney Leadership Consulting Group has created a list of nine guiding behaviors that help to forge good teams. An analysis of these behaviors can serve leaders when working toward building a better team. These behaviors are:

- Acts for the long-term benefit of the company even when it may detract from short-term personal benefits
- Develops positive working relationships with peers
- Supports fellow teammates to succeed
- Involves others in discussing issues and resolving conflicts
- Acknowledges others who demonstrate teamwork
- Informs and involves teammates whenever possible
- Seeks win/win solutions
- Shares information and resources with others
- Credits others for their contributions

Chapter Analysis

Keys to Understanding

- Prioritize teamwork and focus everyone on the importance and benefit of working as a team.
- Reward team players and focus on those working in opposition to the team.
- Teach and encourage employees to engage in behaviors that contribute to teamwork.

Questions for Reflection

1. How do you define a team player?
2. When is it appropriate to work in a team? When is it better to use individual effort?
3. What are the pros and cons of a democratic team versus an autocratic group effort?
4. How can individual effort be recognized in a team environment?
5. How can individual team members be held accountable for their performances?

Chapter 6 Worksheet:
How United Is Your Team?

Yes No

☐ ☐   1.   We get along well; we are respectful and courteous to one another.

☐ ☐   2.   We support each other; we share ideas and opinions openly.

☐ ☐   3.   We respect differences in opinion and give constructive criticism.

☐ ☐   4.   We listen actively to one another, and we communicate effectively.

☐ ☐   5.   We have a common goal; we understand the group's vision and strive to accomplish it collectively.

☐ ☐   6.   We agree on the basic values of the group.

☐ ☐   7.   We give praise to each other and feel free to constructively challenge ideas.

☐ ☐   8.   The group has clear goals and expectations.

☐ ☐   9.   Each member has the necessary equipment, skills, and resources to accomplish a task.

☐ ☐   10. Each member is accountable and responsible for individual actions.

☐ ☐   11. Each person follows through on commitments.

☐ ☐   12. We each support group decisions, even if we voiced concern over them.

☐ ☐   13. We trust each other; we are concerned with the group's success and not just individual success.

**You should have answered yes to at least nine of the questions. If not, you need to look over the questions and determine in which areas your group could improve.

Chapter 7

People Are Watching

A leader is also an actor and must consciously act the part of the leader.

–Alan Axelrod in *Patton on Leadership*

As a leader, people are always watching you, even though in many cases you may be unaware of it. People watch how you dress, how you decorate your office, how you conduct yourself, even where you park your car. While you cannot completely control what others will think of you, you do have the ability to shape their perceptions by how you conduct yourself.

By nature, I am a very logical person. At my office, there are several options for entering the building. I use the seemingly most logical entrance, the door closest to my office. I only have to go through one door, instead of two, as is the case with the other options. I thought nothing about my choice of entry, although I did note that others did not normally use this door.

However, people were taking note of the door I entered and making assumptions about what my choice meant. One of the assumptions was that I was being aloof because I did not choose one of the more commonly used entries to the building. As ridiculous as this may sound, it presents a good example of the fact that as a leader, *people are watching everything you do!*

Although the above assumption had no merit, for some people this perception had become a reality. People don't always behave based upon truth and actual reality. Their behavior is based upon perception and interpretation. Leaders must realize that almost every action they take may be scrutinized, and they should behave accordingly.

There is an old joke that goes: a man jumps off a ten-story building. Do you know what he said for nine floors? He said, "So far, so good." For most people who work in organizations, perception is reality. As a leader you cannot change this. What you can do is recognize it, and when you have a chance, correct misperceptions.

I still come in the same door. I could not bring myself to change my behavior based upon such silliness. As a compromise though, I did try to mention to people my logical reasons for coming in through that door and have on occasion joked about my chosen entry. Sometimes, you just have to let people think what they are going to think. The important concept to understand is that regardless of what you do, people will be watching and drawing conclusions. This does not mean you have to alter your every move, it just means you need to be aware of every move.

You should also be aware of the fact that you, as a leader, represent your company or organization to the outside world. The image that you portray to customers, other companies, and the general public will affect how these people view your organization. Your overall image includes your personality and lifestyle and also how you conduct business. If you are fair, moral, and conscientious, this will reflect back on the organization's reputation. Leaders must be aware of how their actions and words can either jeopardize or benefit their companies.

If you present the qualities of a good leader, professionalism, understanding, dependability, and strength through your actions and speech, you will be perceived that way. You do not have to compromise your basic personality to please everyone, but it is important that you present a persona people can respect. People are more apt to follow willingly and support the visions of a respectable leader. Being aware of all your actions, however minor they seem, helps you to present yourself as the type of high-quality leader you aspire to be.

Chapter Analysis

Keys to Understanding

- Being a leader is like being a celebrity – people are always watching you.

- Be cognizant of your "celebrity" status and work to create positive impact in the organization.

- Allow yourself to be human. You cannot control everyone's perceptions all the time.

Questions for Reflection

1. In what ways do you get feedback about how people perceive you?

2. How are you fulfilling the role of an "actor" in your leadership position?

3. What are the consequences of being perceived incorrectly? In your case, how are perceptions different from reality?

Chapter 8

Pick Your Battles

You can no more win a war than you can an earthquake.

–Jeannette Rankin

I firmly believe in picking your battles. As a leader, you are a limited resource. You have to focus your time and efforts in order to be effective. Sometimes, it is beneficial to stave off a battle or at least defer it for a time. At other times, you need to recognize what is crucially important and fight fiercely for it.

A colleague of mine working at the executive level had a deserved reputation for battling on every issue. This individual was very intelligent, creative, and hardworking, but his inability to pick his battles was his downfall as a leader. Having the capacity to be ferocious when necessary is a good thing, but like anything else, it can be taken to an extreme. If you challenge every issue regardless of its relative importance, people can begin to ignore you when you go on the offensive. You can then become a "boy who cried wolf" leader. This is a sure way to render yourself ineffective.

I believe in a two-fold approach to picking battles. First, you should evaluate the overall importance of the issue. Obviously, the more important the issue, the more reason you have to take it on. Secondly, you should evaluate your chance for success. Some battles you can be reasonably confident that you will win. Others, it may appear that you have little or no chance to succeed. Using this approach, combine the importance of the battle with the chance for success. Only then make your decision on whether or not to take up the fight. It's only common sense to choose important issues in which you have a high probability of succeeding.

If you have a situation that is important but your chance of success is low, you may still want to take on the battle simply because the issue at hand is of paramount significance. Vocalizing and taking action for your core beliefs is an attribute expected of a strong leader. History is full of examples of people who took the lead to champion causes that seemed hopeless. Standing up for others in need and adhering to your sense of justice and morality should not be viewed as a liability, regardless of whether or not you foresee a victory.

There will be times when it is a close call on which action to take. Leaders are called upon to make just these types of difficult decisions. That is why it is so important to have a congruent personal vision, a strong sense of morality, and a view of the situation that encompasses all significant aspects. In deciding upon the right choice, outstanding leaders often consult others, gather all the facts, weigh the relative merits, and then carefully reflect before acting.

Taking a firm stance on an issue should not be intended as a way to showcase your position of authority within an organization. People do not like being dominated simply for the feeling of power it gives their leader. This only alienates them. Choosing battles that improve or benefit the organization is what you should be focusing on. Being proven "right" is not the most important issue. Creating divisions or rifts within the group out of arrogance is not a healthy approach to leadership. You must seek to bring unity and consensus to your organization.

A final note on battles comes from Secretary of State Colin Powell. His philosophy on the use of military force has been referred to as the "Powell Doctrine." Its essence is that force should be used as a last resort. If, however, it becomes clear that force must be used, it should be used in an over-whelming fashion. If you decide to take on a battle, don't do it with a half-hearted drive or energy. If you are taking on an issue for the overall good of the organization, then play to win!

Chapter Analysis

Keys to Understanding

- Pick your battles based upon importance and probability for success.

- Sometimes, it is more important to build consensus than to be "right."

- When you decide to battle, fight with strength and conviction.

Questions for Reflection

1. When have you avoided a battle that involved your core beliefs? What was the outcome? Would you have done it differently given the chance?

2. Do you perceive "building consensus" to always be the best approach? Think about people you know who are consensus builders. Are they successful?

3. Where do you draw the line between fighting for what you believe is right and arrogance?

48 The Call to Lead

Accomplish More by Doing Less

A jack of all trades is king of none.

–P.K. Thomajan

*It is not enough to be busy; so are the ants.
The question is: what are we busy about?*

–Henry David Thoreau

I once worked for an organization that had a leader with a major problem. This individual had great difficulty prioritizing organizational goals and objectives. When asked what the top priorities were, he would maintain that everything was equally as important. This was a real problem, because people need a leader who possesses a clear set of priorities. Taking the approach that everything is equally as important creates confusion. In reality, if everything is important, then nothing has any priority. A leader who fails to help employees prioritize assignments is creating a potentially dangerous situation. The resulting confusion can rapidly lead to fatigue and staff burnout.

Good employees are able to effectively manage multiple responsibilities, but there is a breaking point. Good leaders almost instinctively feel when this is near and shift or alter priorities accordingly. This requires insight into your staff and your organization. Communicating with and getting to know workers helps you to identify where individual strengths and weaknesses lie. Having clear goals and ideas on how to accomplish them lets you judge your priorities and when they can be adjusted.

There are habits you can form to help you prioritize tasks. Make daily "to-do" lists. High-priority items should be placed at the top and marked off when completed. You may even want to make a separate list of on-going, low-priority items and refer to it weekly. You can also make a list of your larger goals and then create a plan on how to achieve them. Making some type of visual diagram or list of steps to accomplishing your goal may help you stay focused. These organizational tools help you see the "big picture" and prioritize objectives.

When prioritizing, there are a few things to keep in mind. First, you must decide when the thing must be finished. This will help you determine its priority and break down any initial steps you need to accomplish first. Secondly, you need to consider the importance of the goal. It's at this point that you should consider whether or not this is a task that can be delegated. Delegation can free some of your time and allow you to really focus on the high-priority objectives.

I have always believed in the notion of doing fewer things better. Even a very large corporation like General Electric never has more than five major initiatives going on at any one time. It is their belief that having more than a few chosen priorities will result in a house divided. Good leaders create top priorities and continually evaluate them. This allows employees to focus on what is important. Staff members have more focus and less stress when they understand the priorities.

There may be times when you cannot fully commit to accomplishing certain tasks or projects. When this occurs, you should hold off on them. Do not initiate a project when you cannot give your full attention to it. Priorities should only be established when there is a full organizational commitment to accomplishing them.

A scene from the movie, *The Karate Kid,* helps to illustrate this point:

Karate student Daniel arrives for his first lesson. The old master asks him if he is ready. Daniel says, "I guess so." His teacher explains to him that the proper answer is either karate yes or karate no. Never is it karate "I guess so." His teacher tells him that karate requires a full commitment. If you cannot make such a commitment, then do not pursue karate. Daniel understands the lesson and answers that he is ready.

Unfortunately, many leaders have failed to understand this lesson. They make many "I guess so" commitments on behalf of the organization. Leaders should make every effort to avoid this. If you cannot bring your full attention and energy to a project, you cannot expect your employees to do so.

Chapter Analysis

Keys to Understanding

- Set clear priorities and continually articulate them.
- If priorities change, let people know right away. If possible, share any reasoning behind the changes.
- Consider doing fewer things better.

Questions for Reflection

1. How many priorities do you have?

2. How many tasks that you have on your to-do list could be delegated?

3. How often do you communicate your priorities to those that work for you? How often are your boss's priorities made clear to you?

Accountability

No individual raindrop ever considers itself responsible for the flood.

−Anonymous

It's a sad day when you find out that it's not accident or time or fortune but just yourself that kept things from you.

−Lillian Hellman

We have become a society of victims, with very little responsibility focused on one's own conduct. Whenever something goes wrong, it seems it is always someone else's fault. Extreme examples include:

- The burglar who fell through a roof and sued the property owner for failure to properly maintain the roof.

- A man competed in a strongman competition in which he ran a 40-yard dash with a refrigerator strapped to his back. He was injured and sued the manufacturer of the refrigerator for failing to post a sign on it warning people that it was hazardous to run a race with the appliance strapped to their backs.

This trend is not completely new, as evidenced by this story about former New York Yankee Yogi Berra. One afternoon, he swung at three very wide pitches in succession and struck out. He returned to the dugout shaking his head. The other players sat waiting for an outburst of self-blame.

Instead, Berra, addressing no one in particular, muttered, "How does a pitcher like that stay in the league?"

Police officers are held to a higher standard due to the position they hold in society. They are accountable for their actions on-duty as well as off-duty. This higher standard applies to leaders as well. The higher you are in an organization, the more responsibility is expected of you. Some leaders fail to see this. They think that their high positions give them more leeway in how they can conduct themselves.

As leaders, we must hold people accountable, but it must begin with ourselves. Whenever a mistake is made that can even remotely be traced to our actions, we must accept responsibility. This sets an example for everyone else in the organization to do the same. If the leaders do not encourage this through their own behavior, they will likely not see the behavior they desire in others. Lead by your own example.

The most common mistake leaders make in this area is to voice the importance of accountability without holding themselves accountable at every turn. If this is your action as a leader, I can guarantee that people will notice, and they will be inclined to follow your actions, not your words.

Ultimately, when it comes to the organization, the leader is accountable for everything. When a problem or crisis arises, the leader is the first person looked to regardless of whether or not they are the one personally responsible. No matter who is at fault, the leader will be given (by customers, clients, and employees) the task of acknowledging the situation and solving the problem. Transferring blame will only lessen your image. What a good leader does is accept responsibility, correct the current situation as much as possible, and take preventative measures to ensure that the same mistake does not happen again.

If you require a certain behavior from yourself, it is easier for you to require it from others. Everyone should be accountable for the actions that they take. This is not a blame game at all, and in fact, people should be recognized and at times rewarded for taking responsibility for something that went awry. At the least, you want to create an environment where people can feel comfortable admitting mistakes. No one necessarily likes to do this, and it is important that they do not fear a hostile reaction.

Chapter Analysis

Keys to Understanding

- First and foremost, hold yourself accountable.

- Hold your people accountable but support them to the greatest degree possible when they make mistakes.

Questions for Reflection

1. How often do you seek to avoid responsibility for an outcome by placing blame on someone else?

2. How do you hold people responsible for their actions?

3. What is the "culture" of you organization in regards to accountability?

Chapter 11

Determination and Adversity

Some people succeed because they are destined to succeed, but most succeed because they are determined to succeed.

–Winston Churchill

Adversity introduces a man to himself.

–Anonymous

Determination is perhaps the key to success in any endeavor, and the field of leadership is no different. In order to achieve the greatest level of organizational success, leaders must display determination in everything that they do. Most importantly, employees tend to take on the characteristics of their leaders. If leaders are determined to succeed despite all obstacles, employees will see this and learn that tenacity is an important ingredient of success. An organization full of determined leaders and employees is a formidable force indeed.

Employees need you to display determination even when you are uncertain. If you give up as soon as things look difficult, it sends the message that when the going gets tough, it is acceptable to give up. If your goals are not worth struggle and effort, what's the point? Why should anyone care if they are realized or not? Your determination motivates employees to struggle for what is important even if it involves hardship. You will increase their enthusiasm, and they will probably view you with more respect and admiration.

Modeling determination for employees is even more important in times of adversity. Leaders are closely watched at all times but particularly during stressful times. People want to see that their leaders are strong and determined in crisis situations. Leaders are nothing if not providers of hope, determination, and tenacity.

Leaders should be very visible in the organization in times of adversity. This is certainly not the time to stay in the office behind the desk. People want assurance that everything will be worked out, and it is the leader's job to provide that assurance. This is not to say that a leader is required to sugar-coat tough issues. To the contrary, people appreciate a leader who is open and honest about the circumstances. However, they also want a leader who has the ability to give them hope just when all seems hopeless.

It is interesting to note what happens when there is an unusual noise or severe turbulence during an airplane flight. Experienced fliers immediately look to the flight attendants for any clue of distress. If there is none, comfort levels increase. This is the calmness a leader can give an organization when crisis occurs. People watch their leaders. They want to see quiet confidence coupled with a good grasp of the facts. They want to see determination, and they want to feel hope. Good leaders really earn their money during tough times.

Perseverance may seem something inborn, not something you can learn. However, I believe that you can develop your determination. It takes confidence and a positive attitude to face uncertainty and possible failure and still be determined to push on. If you are genuine, have a strong vision, and are committed to your goals, it is easier to stay focused and not let doubts erode your confidence. It is at these times that a strong faith in yourself, your vision, the corporate vision, and your organization and people is crucial. Such faith will give you the confidence that you need.

It is important to maintain a balance between determination and stubbornness. You should not give in at every obstacle, but you should not hold out when it is painfully obvious that nothing is going to be accomplished. You may be thinking of "saving face" by not admitting defeat or you may be worried that failure will expose you as incapable, but it is important that you know "when to say when." There will be times when it is simply necessary to end a project because it is no longer productive or possible to continue. In these cases, it is better to quit gracefully than to drag everyone through a pointless and unpleasant situation. The art of leadership includes knowing when to advance despite the odds and realizing when a strategic retreat is the wisest course of action.

Chapter Analysis

Keys to Understanding

- Leaders should set the tone and create an environment in which people are encouraged to be determined in their efforts.

- During times of trouble, leaders should be very active and visible.

Questions for Reflection

1. Reflect upon times of crisis; how did the leaders you reported to respond? Did they show determination and calm during the period of crisis? How did their response affect those around them?

2. How do leaders "set the tone" in an organization? What "small things" are noticed?

3. How do you communicate determination and hope?

Chapter 12

When the Cat Is Away...

The final test of a leader is that he leaves behind him in other men the conviction and the will to carry on.

–Walter Lippmann

My proudest moments as a leader have been when I have returned from an extended absence. Some people think this is odd, but I do not. In my mind, the most important duty I have as a leader is to mentor and develop people to accomplish organizational goals even when I am not around. When I return and everything is running smoothly, I'm as proud as I can be. To me, this means that I have properly prepared people to succeed in my absence. Further, should I leave the organization for some reason, I have trained people to replace me.

I once worked for a boss who evidently did not feel this way. When he left me in charge in his absence for the first time, I took pride in ensuring that everything was taken care of and handled effectively. Upon his return, although he did not say so, it was clear that he was not happy that things had gone so well during his absence.

After observing him and thinking about it for some time, I came to the conclusion that he had a feeling of not being needed. He did not feel comfortable thinking the organization could run well without him. Although I felt this was a weakness of his, I was sensitive to his feelings. It's proof that problems can arise when you let your ego dictate how you lead your organization.

The next time he was gone, although I took care of everything important, I left a couple of minor things unattended. Upon his return, I pointed these things out and sought his guidance on how to proceed. He responded favorably to this tactic, and that is how I handled him from that point on.

Under optimum conditions, I should not have had to do this. However, as is often the case in life, optimum conditions are not always present. As a leader, be proud if your people have done well in your absence. It does not mean that they do not need you; it means you are probably doing a good job as a leader.

Chapter Analysis

Keys to Understanding

- Work hard to prepare people to perform competently in your absence.

- Take note of how things went in your absence. It is one of the truest gauges of how well you are doing in your role as a leader.

Questions for Reflection

1. Do you secretly wish that things will not run smoothly when you are away? If so, what feelings, thoughts, or insecurities are leading you to feel this way?

2. What steps have you taken to train your people to deal with matters in your absence?

3. If your organization ran fine without you present, then why are you needed?

Chapter
13

Surround Yourself with Excellence

The best executive is one who has sense enough to pick good men to do what he wants done and self-restraint enough to keep from meddling with them while they do it.

–Theodore Roosevelt

In my view, the only way to create an excellent organization is to hire the best people available. There are many companies with great equipment, good training, good management, and clearly defined goals. However, these are relatively meaningless if you don't have top-notch people.

In order to hire the best, you have to recruit accordingly. Immense effort should be put into finding and selecting people who have the potential to be outstanding employees. Self-evaluation and evaluation of the current employees and organization is needed in order to hire wisely. The boss must know where the strengths and weaknesses of the organization are and the dynamics that will help it reach its highest potential. You should hire people who fit the group's style and who can complement the skills of the rest of the organization. You should not be hasty when it comes to selecting your employees. In the long run, it will save you time and resources to carefully select the best people, even though it may seem a difficult and arduous process.

Once employees are hired, it is important to focus on training and evaluating them extensively during their first year.

This period is actually the last, and most important, part of the selection process.

You have to be almost ruthless in your approach to probationary employees. People should be expected to excel during this period. This is probably when you will get the best effort and attitude from them. If they are marginal at this point, the chances of them improving after they pass the probationary period are slim. Although it is conceptually possible, never in my career have I seen someone who was below average during probation go on to become an outstanding performer.

Once you are satisfied with the people you have hired and trained, it is important that you let them know that they are valued. Great employees are priceless additions to your organization. No matter how outstanding the leader is, an organization will never thrive without the work and dedication of an excellent staff.

Hiring the Right Candidate

Hiring new employees is an important job that requires a great deal of thought and evaluation. Here are some questions to ask yourself when considering new candidates for employment:

✓ Do they have strengths and skills that your organization lacks?

✓ What are their areas of weakness, and how will these affect their job performances?

✓ Do they fit with the group's work style?

✓ How do their work histories demonstrate their abilities?

✓ How much training do they need, and is it available?

✓ Do they have good attitudes and interpersonal skills?

✓ What are their ambitions within the organization?

Chapter Analysis

Keys to Understanding

- Spare no effort or expense in hiring and training the right people.

- Insist on excellence during the probationary period. It is the most important part of the selection process.

Questions for Reflection

1. How do you evaluate an employee during the probationary period? How is it different from the way in which you evaluate a long-term employee?

2. How do you train new employees so that they can succeed?

3. How can you differentiate between performance issues and becoming acclimated to the organization?

4. What is unique or different about your hiring practices that encourages or promotes the selection of the best candidates?

Chapter 13 Worksheet: Employee Evaluation

Yes No

☐ ☐ 1. Works well with coworkers; shares ideas and assists others.

☐ ☐ 2. Understands organization's or group's vision and objectives and strives to accomplish them.

☐ ☐ 3. Listens to others and communicates effectively.

☐ ☐ 4. Contributes positive, useful ideas to the group.

☐ ☐ 5. Meets deadlines.

☐ ☐ 6. Has a good attendance record.

☐ ☐ 7. Quality of work is high; errors are kept to a minimum.

☐ ☐ 8. Continues to develop and learn new skills.

☐ ☐ 9. Has initiative and is able to work with minimal supervision.

☐ ☐ 10. Recognizes problems, both actual and potential, and solves them proactively.

☐ ☐ 11. Recognizes errors or weaknesses and strives to correct them; can take constructive criticism.

☐ ☐ 12. Follows guidelines but is also imaginative and innovative.

☐ ☐ 13. Has a positive, cooperative attitude.

☐ ☐ 14. Is self-motivated.

** You should have answered yes to at least ten of these questions regarding your employee.

Chapter
14

Consensus

You can employ men and hire hands to work for you, but you must win their hearts to have them work with you.

—William Boetcker

Leaders have the right to do what they feel is best for the organization. The smart leader, however, involves people in decisions and attempts to gain consensus whenever possible. Communicating your visions and goals and clearly outlining directions are keys to successful leadership, but listening to your employees is also very important. Paying attention to the feedback and ideas that your staff provides works to your advantage. There are two main reasons for this.

First, employees working at the scene of the action are generally going to know more about what is currently happening than their organizational superiors. Not many bosses like to admit it, but the smart ones know this to be true. Good leaders rely upon their trusted workers to give them up-to-the-minute information and feedback. They use this information when forming decisions on how to proceed. Also, this communicates trust and respect for employees, one of the most important messages any leader can send to workers. It lets them know that you value and respect their work.

Secondly, when you gain consensus, people are personally invested in the initiative. A leader can tell people what to do without asking them, and they will most likely make an effort toward compliance. However, when people are actively involved in creating the direction, their commitment to it increases enormously. When possible, collaboration with your employees creates numerous benefits. It makes the project more personal for them, and it may bring new perspectives or ideas to a situation. This is the type of involvement and consensus that helps to create success in an organization.

I had a boss once who had a disastrous approach to gaining consensus. He would hold staff meetings and discuss specifically how he wanted to handle each issue. Only after going on record with his position would he ask for input. Obviously, this inhibited feedback as he had already made it clear what he thought was the best approach to each issue. In one case, he went so far as to say he would be damned if we were going to do things any way other than the way he had described. Then, as usual, he asked for input on how we should handle this issue! He had obviously not realized the importance of employee feedback and certainly did not know how to go about gathering it.

Another time, I had a phony consensus builder for a boss. Here is an example of his approach: there was an important community member who had a pet project that involved the use of police resources. Our leader made a commitment to the person that they would have the department's support. After doing this, it would have been career suicide for the leader to back out.

Rather than informing the department of the project we would be involved in, he created a committee. He went before the committee and explained what the project entailed. He said the department would not be involved in the project unless there was consensus in the group. He ended by asking what we thought and whether or not we wanted to do the project. Based upon his position in the organization, no one felt comfortable turning him down, but many people in the room felt that the process was a charade. In many people's view, his integrity was compromised.

Leaders do not fool people when they engage in false consensus building. Where the direction is a foregone conclusion, such as in the above example, why toy with people? It reflects a lack of respect for your employees and their basic intelligence. A better approach is to let them know what needs to be done and then allow them input into how to accomplish the job in question. Their respect for you as a leader and a person of integrity is worth being honest with them.

Chapter Analysis

Keys to Understanding

- Invest resources in building consensus. It is well worth the time and effort.

- Whenever something must be done, don't engage in a consensus-building ruse. Instead, tell people what must be done and allow them to help determine how to accomplish the task.

Questions for Reflection

1. What kind of feedback do your employees give you? Do you really know what's going on?

2. How do you use feedback to get consensus?

3. Do you feel that consensus building is an important part of your management style?

4. How do you handle disagreement or criticism within a group that is working to reach consensus?

5. In what types of situations do you feel that it is important to gain a group consensus?

Lifelong Learning

A person is not old until regrets take the place of dreams.

–John Barrymore

*The man who graduates today and stops learning tomorrow
is uneducated the day after.*

–Newton Baker

Education and learning have become extremely important. Leaders are expected to have knowledge and expertise; your people look to you for answers. If you are going to be effective, you need to be involved in on-going learning. Things are changing at a breakneck pace, and it is difficult to stay completely current. Part of your responsibility as a leader is to constantly strive to keep your knowledge as up to date as possible.

Being a lifelong learner has gone from being an option to being a necessity. There are a variety of different ways leaders can do this. Formal education, training courses, independent reading, and networking with other leaders are all excellent methods. No matter what route you take, be sure that you pursue a path to stay versed in new developments, ideas, or technologies that may be beneficial to the organization.

Most organizations want their employees to be lifelong learners as well. Again, it starts with the leader. If the leader is constantly striving to learn, this will encourage the employees; they will see it as part of what the organization requires. The benefits of having knowledgeable employees who continue to learn are immense, and the effects will continue to ripple throughout the organization.

Chapter Analysis

Keys to Understanding

- As a leader, you should constantly strive to educate yourself.

- Leaders who model this behavior end up with "learning organizations" that are full of people who are lifelong learners.

Questions for Reflection

1. Do you have personal education and career-development plans for each of your employees?

2. What is your own personal lifelong learning strategy?

3. How does your organization approach the task of staying current in technology, news and changes in your field, and skill developments?

4. Do you have any ideas to improve upon your organization's approach to creating a "learning organization?"

Chapter 16

Dependability

You can't build a reputation on what you are going to do.

—Henry Ford

Magnificent promises are always to be suspected.

—Theodore Parker

Dependability is saying what you will do and doing what you say. Leaders must have an impeccable reputation for dependability. It is critical that your bosses, peers, and subordinates all feel that you can be relied on to follow up your words with actions.

I faced an awkward situation once when a boss instructed me to enter into a negotiation with another public agency and reach an arrangement agreeable to all. Through some hard work and a little bit of finesse, I was able to reach a good agreement in which both parties got what they wanted.

After I had drafted the agreement for my boss's signature, he explained that he no longer wanted to participate. A very frank discussion between the two of us ensued, but I was forced to contact the other party and tell them that there would be no deal. What an uncomfortable position to be put in, especially since there was no identifiable reason for the reversed decision. It was as if he had changed his mind on a whim.

I never again believed this boss to be dependable, and my interactions with him reflected this. From that point on, I was very cautious when dealing with him, and I always held his integrity suspect. As a leader, when you make a commitment, you must live up to it.

At the very least, if circumstances change and you cannot complete the commitment, explain in detail to those involved why the change occurred. Even if they are upset about the situation, they will be more understanding and retain their respect for you. Needless to say, you should only break obligations under very pressing circumstances. This is why it is so important to think through the situation before you commit. Too many leaders find themselves over-committing and then scrambling to get out of their obligations later.

You should be cautious and conservative in making commitments. Think it through and do not act based solely on your first reaction or your desire to please. People will remember for a long time the commitments you keep. More lasting, however, will be the impressions left by the commitments you failed to meet. If you have over-committed and don't have the time or resources to do a job well, you will disappoint everyone involved – including yourself.

Being dependable is directly tied to your integrity. If your employees cannot depend on you, your reputation will evaporate. It becomes difficult to work for a boss whose word is essentially useless. Some workers will feel that they do not have to work as hard at objectives because an un-reliable boss may just dismiss the task in the end. Others will suffer because the managerial support they need is lacking. Others will take their cues from the leader and feel content to be undependable themselves. An unreliable leader causes the cohesion, organization, and productivity of the organization to decline.

Chapter Analysis

Keys to Understanding

- Dependability is a key trait for leaders.

- Make commitments cautiously, after careful thought and evaluation.

- If conditions change and you absolutely cannot keep a commitment, let people know as soon as possible. If appropriate, let them know why the change was necessary.

Questions for Reflection

1. Do you find that commitments you make must often be changed, extended, or broken? What factors contribute to this?

2. Managers report that personal or family commitments are the ones that are most often changed or broken due to work "priorities." Do you experience this in your life? What are the effects?

3. Do those that make commitments to you sometimes fail to deliver on time? How does that make you evaluate them? What factors contribute to this? What can you do as a leader to change these patterns?

4. Do you often feel pressured to make commitments that are impossible or difficult to meet? Is this used as a manipulative ploy? How can you change the situation?

Chapter 17

Recognizing Weakness

Experience is very valuable. It keeps a man who makes the same mistake twice from admitting it the third time.

–Brook Benton

We have all probably come in contact with people who think that they have all the answers. What passes for complete arrogance is often an attempt to hide immense insecurity and self-doubt. When leaders act as if they have all the answers and are free from any weaknesses, those around them suffer from the charade, and sometimes the company can be at jeopardy.

No one should expect perfection from themselves or others. What is important though is that you recognize your weaknesses and not try to cover them up. Instead, seek self-knowledge and then compensate or correct the weaknesses. Some people are good at identifying their weaknesses while most of us are not. How do you identify your weaknesses? If you evaluate your own performance, you can become aware of some points. They are the easy ones. What is difficult is identifying weaknesses that you can't see. One way is to ask your superior, a peer, or your own workers for an assessment. This can be a delicate situation; some will be forthcoming when you ask, but many will not. Some of what they say may be valuable, some may be a pure putdown or spurious. Regardless, you will gain valuable insight that will help you evaluate yourself.

Some organizations are now using formal "360-degree" assessments on their leaders. Such an assessment requires that superiors, peers, and subordinates all evaluate management personnel. This concept takes feedback beyond the standard evaluation you may receive from your boss. Peers and subordinates will have their own perspective regarding a leader's performance. Compiling information in this "360-degree" fashion creates a much more diverse and comprehensive evaluation of one's performance. Part of the process is also a self-evaluation. This will show how you are doing versus how you *think* you are doing. All this information is compiled and shared with the leader in an effort to improve performance.

Identifying weaknesses requires honest self-assessment. People who have gotten to a leadership position are usually strong, confident individuals, so it may be hard for them to admit that they cannot do something well or that they need help in a certain area. You must keep in mind that being the best leader you can is going to require continual work. As in many areas of life, natural talent will only take you so far; you must learn and practice to rise to the top.

Assessment also requires that you have the ability to critically listen to others when they give you input. It is difficult to hear criticism without getting angry or becoming defensive. Here again, the natural confidence that got you the leadership position in the first place may cause trouble. Never let yourself fall into the trap of believing that no one has anything to teach you or that you alone come up with the best ways to do things. Be open to the suggestions of others, even when these suggestions deal with your own performance. Show your employees that it is beneficial to take healthy criticism by being the one to model this behavior.

On the other hand, be careful in how you interpret such criticism. If you appear too eager for feedback, peers, bosses, and subordinates alike may perceive you to be weak, indecisive, and lacking in self-confidence. Getting feedback about your performance when you are the leader is a delicate operation.

As you identify weaknesses, you have to assess whether it makes sense to devote effort to rectifying them or whether you can just as well compensate for them. For example, a leader who has no knowledge of financial analysis may find it better to have a good analyst on staff rather than go through the struggle of attempting to become a financial expert. Sometimes, it may be a joint effort: compensating in part while you get up to speed on the basics.

Once you have identified your weak points that you are going to remedy, do not put off implementing a plan for improving them. For example, I realized that I had very poor computer skills, and I knew that I should strengthen my knowledge in this area. I bought a laptop computer, attended instructional courses, and read all of the *Computers for Dummies* books I could find. I made a lot of progress, but there were a couple of times when, in my frustration, I almost ended up tossing the computer out the window. Ultimately, I became proficient. Now I present my leadership and career-development seminars using a fancy PowerPoint presentation, something I would not have thought possible several years ago.

An interesting side note is that now people in my organization come to me with some of their computer problems. They seem to think that I know what I'm doing, and incredibly, many times I am able to help them. I must say that making a feared weakness into a strong skill is one of the most rewarding things you can do.

As you identify and come to know your weak areas, you need to surround yourself with people who help to balance them. It is human nature to select those just like you, but the smart leaders intentionally pick a variety of people so that they get an overall balance of strengths and weaknesses. Surrounding yourself with exceptional people reduces the likelihood that a weakness will cause a problem. No single person is going to be able to give the organization everything it needs. When you have others around who excel where you are weakest, you can focus on what you really do best. Organizations with diversified staffs succeed because they have the ability to meet any challenge.

Chapter Analysis

Keys to Understanding

- Determine a system whereby you can evaluate your own strengths and weaknesses. Pick one at a time and work on it until it is no longer a weak area.

- Surround yourself with people who bring strength to areas that are not your forte.

Questions for Reflection

1. Do you feel that assessment by your subordinates would erode your managerial authority?

2. When did you last prepare a list of areas for improvement? What happened to the list?

3. What are the relative advantages and disadvantages of a formal review versus an informal system?

4. Do you have any plan in the works that will help you to improve one of your weak areas? If so, how are you progressing?

Chapter 18

Saying No

It is a great evil, as well as a misfortune, to be unable to utter a prompt and decided "no."

−Charles Simmons

One of the most difficult bosses I have worked for was incapable of saying no, even when he wanted to. He would go to immense lengths to avoid having to say no. His first technique was to simply not give an answer, until the person or group quit asking. His second defense was to set up obstacles so that it would be impossible to accomplish what was desired. This caused people to give up; it became more trouble than it was worth. His final strategy was to actually say yes and then work behind the scenes to sabotage the project.

I think he had trouble saying no because he wanted to be popular, and it is hard to be popular when you are the one saying no. I also think that he just didn't have the fortitude. He found it was easier to employ his little evasive strategies, which in effect resulted in a no answer. The "advantage" of this was that he got his desired result without having to deny anyone.

To add insult to injury, when the issue invariably came up again, he would always be sure to let everyone know that he had not turned down the request when it had come up the first time. Did he really believe that he was fooling anyone? These sorts of game players usually end up using their "moves" so often that everyone in the organization eventually knows exactly what is going on. What's more, they end up losing what they craved the most: respect, popularity, and admiration.

As a leader, when the answer is no, say so! Be decisive and give a clear and resounding no. Although people may not initially care for your response, in the long run they will accept it. Employees would rather hear a firm no than an insincere yes. They want the full support and backing of their leader. If you are not able to give this, then say no in the beginning.

Explain the reasoning behind your answer if at all possible. Do it in a matter-of-fact way. Do not be apologetic about it, or you may come across as weak. Be sure employees understand why you are giving them the explanation. When you explain your reasoning, you communicate respect, and it helps the person to accept the decision better. Also, the more employees understand the reasons actions are taken, the greater they develop their depth of organizational understanding. You actually engage in a form of training, helping your employees to be prepared to assume more responsibility when the need arises.

Chapter Analysis

Keys to Understanding

- Try to make sure that you have the facts straight before you make a decision.
- If the answer is no, do not be afraid to say it.
- Explain the reasoning behind the answer if possible.

Questions for Reflection

1. When do you have a hard time saying no?
2. Is your organization predisposed to quick yes-no answers, or does it encourage drawn-out decision making?
3. How often do your decisions include "why" in the answer? What about the answers that you receive?

Logic

Logic plays a very important role in the workplace and in life in general. Usually, when logic is applied to leadership issues, the results are good decisions and effective actions. Logic-based leadership is only possible when you look at the "big picture" in an organization. If you do not have a clear view of where you would like to lead your company, it is difficult to make decisions, face change, communicate with workers, or balance competing concerns. You must have a strong vision statement and a firm grasp of organizational policies. Otherwise, facing challenges from a logical perspective will be very difficult.

This section addresses certain concepts that are primarily grounded in logic. There are twelve leadership areas that can be positively impacted with logic. As with the other two components, this section is not designed to be freestanding. It should be blended with common sense and concern for people. Only when all three components are present can you be a truly effective leader.

Chapter
19

The Importance of Failure

Failure is only the opportunity to begin again more intelligently.

–Henry Ford

In great attempts, it is glorious even to fail.

–Cassius Longinus

Winston Churchill flunked the sixth grade. Albert Einstein was four years old before he could speak and seven before he could read. When Thomas Edison was a boy, his teachers told him that he was too stupid to learn anything. A newspaper fired Walt Disney because he had "no good ideas." Beethoven's music teacher once said of him that as a composer, he was hopeless.

The list of "failures" goes on and on. Failure is perhaps the first greatest key to success. More specifically, it is how you respond to failure that is the real key. Growth in an organization only comes with stretching and risk taking. When trying something new, mistakes are inevitable. It is up to the leader to create a healthy environment where people are not afraid to fail. Mistakes should be seen as an integral part of the organizational process. They are a normal part of striving for excellence.

Obviously, some mistakes are easier to tolerate than others. Action should be taken when a mistake is made, but ordinarily, it should be corrective action, not censure. Mistakes present a unique opportunity to teach and develop your staff. Growth and success cannot come without risk taking, and progress does not occur without mistakes.

As a leader, one of the ways I approach errors is judging whether I feel the mistake was a "mistake of the heart" or a "mistake of the head." A mistake of the heart is a situation where an employee intentionally did something that was known to be wrong and tried to get away with it. I tend to be very harsh in such situations. A mistake of the head occurs when an employee is working hard to do the right thing, but for some reason, it does not work out that way. I tend to be very lenient on these types of mistakes. In fact, there have been times when I have actually praised one of my people for a mistake because their intentions were so good.

If you chastise or punish employees for every mistake, their focus will be on self-preservation not on striving for excellence. Instead of working to succeed, they will work to avoid censure or failure. These two approaches are vastly different. People working to avoid harsh criticism will do the least amount possible. They will show very little initiative and creativity and will rarely do anything without authorization from the boss. They will shirk from accepting responsibility, look for reasons to assert that it isn't their job, and in general act like inefficient bureaucrats. Mistakes may be avoided, but it comes at the cost of overall organizational success.

The goal of a leader is not to avoid all possible failures. It is to avoid errors that can be easily foreseen, as well as risks that are not worth the potential costs. Good leaders are willing to take risks in order to improve their operations. If you never try anything new, you cannot possibly hope to improve. Expect that failure is usually the result the first time you try anything. It is how you learn from your failure that counts.

Consider this man's life story:

- Failed in business at age 22
- Ran for legislature - defeated at age 23
- Again failed in business at age 24
- Elected to legislature at age 25
- Had a nervous breakdown at age 27
- Defeated for Speaker at age 29
- Defeated for Elector at age 31
- Defeated for Congress at age 34
- Elected to Congress at age 37
- Defeated for Congress at age 39
- Defeated for Senate at age 46
- Defeated for Vice President at age 47
- Defeated for Senate at age 49
- Elected President of the United States at age 51

This is the life and career record of Abraham Lincoln.

Steps to Success

No one likes to fail. So, how can you avoid it? Here are some steps you can take to help you achieve success:

- ✓ Clearly define your goal(s).
- ✓ Write a detailed plan of how to accomplish your goal(s).
- ✓ Be decisive; don't procrastinate once you make a plan.
- ✓ Be a lifelong learner. You must continue to obtain new knowledge and skills.
- ✓ Do not quit because you see failure as a possibility. Have courage in the face of adversity.
- ✓ If you make mistakes, acknowledge your responsibility.
- ✓ Learn from your errors and do not let failure stop you.
- ✓ Be open to feedback and criticism.

These steps should be shared with your employees as well. Encourage them to make goals and to take appropriate risks. Support them in this approach by handling the results appropriately. Move your organization away from bureaucracy and toward entrepreneurial enthusiasm.

◊

Success is the ability to go from one failure to the next with great enthusiasm.
—Winston Churchill
◊

Chapter Analysis

Keys to Understanding

- Let your employees know that it is acceptable, and at times even beneficial, to make intelligent errors.

- To the greatest extent possible, be gentle with people when they have failed.

- Use failure as a springboard to success.

Questions for Reflection

1. How do you distinguish between corrective action and censure when faced with an employee who made a mistake?

2. How do you encourage working for success instead of working to avoid failure?

3. How do you handle a situation in which a well-meaning employee makes a mistake of judgment?

4. How have you learned from failures in your life?

Communication

When you talk, you repeat what you already know; when you listen, you often learn something.

–Jared Sparks

I believe that effective communication is the most challenging issue that any organization faces. It is a never-ending process and one in which the effectiveness is difficult to measure. As a result, it is easy to become complacent and believe that everything is all right when in fact the situation may be critical. There is little feedback until things go awry. Even leaders who are constantly vigilant regularly fail in this area. For large companies that are geographically spread out, the problem is even greater. It can also be difficult to give feedback for companies on a single site, particularly if you have employees on different shifts and different schedules. Invariably, it seems somebody didn't "get the word."

An example of this happening is shown in the story told below:

The great director Cecil B. DeMille was making one of his grand epic movies. He had six cameras at various points to pick up all the overall action and five other cameras set up to film plot developments involving the major characters. At 6:00 a.m., the large cast had begun rehearsing the scene. They went through it four times, and it was now late afternoon. The sun was setting; there was just enough light to get the shot done. DeMille looked over the panorama, saw that all was right, and gave the command for action. One hundred extras charged up the hill; another hundred came down the same hill to do mock battle. In another location, 200 extras labored to move a huge stone into place. After 15 minutes of non-stop action, DeMille yelled, "Cut," and he told his assistants that he was very pleased with the action. He waved to the camera crew supervisor to ensure that all the cameras had picked up what they had been assigned to film. From the top of the hill, the camera supervisor waved back, raised his megaphone, and called out, "Ready when you are CB!"

This story is not too far off from what is happening every day in organizations. Even in companies that have good communication, problems always arise. One of the common methods leaders use to positively impact communications is the "open-door policy." This ordinarily means that any employee can come in and talk with a top-level boss, without navigating through the hierarchy. I have always had an open-door policy, but there are some cautions to its use.

First, you have to ensure that the employee is not "shopping" for an answer to their concern. If workers have already gotten an answer that they object to from a lower-level boss, the worker should share that with you. Sometimes employees are not forthcoming with this information, and you have to be responsible for seeking that out. Secondly, the bosses under you may not be happy that their employees have direct access to someone at a higher level. They may feel that their authority is being threatened, and you should be sensitive to these concerns.

Warren Bennis, author of *Managing People is like Herding Cats*, has an open-door policy, but his rule is that he will not give a decision without conferring with lower-level bosses to get their perspective on the situation. I think this is a good approach and works to balance the needs of the employees with support for supervision and management.

Perhaps the most important and sadly the most neglected part of communication is active listening. Years ago, I had a boss who would not give me his full attention when I spoke to him. Although it was not intentional, it was very distracting when he would answer the phone, shuffle through his desk, and even clip his nails while I was speaking to him. Leaders should give their full attention when someone is speaking. If you cannot actively listen to an employee at a particular time, simply make arrangements to talk with that person later. Actively listening to people is one of the best ways to convey your respect for them.

Active listening requires a great deal of effort and patience. Often times, people make snap judgments about a person's perspective on things before they even have a conversation. This makes effective communication more difficult. To truly understand a person's view, we must actively listen to what they are trying to get across. Asking questions or paraphrasing what the person has said are good ways to make sure that you are understanding, and not just "hearing," what is being said. If you avoid interrupting and give the speaker your full attention, you will earn their respect. You will be in a better position to ask questions after the speaker is through, and you will avoid hearing an exasperated person say, "I was just getting to that."

On the other hand, we have all known people who can talk on and on without making a point. An astute leader should gauge the tempo of a conversation and know how to "speed it along" to get to the main points. An adroit leader should master the art of moving a conversation along gracefully and ending it gracefully.

Good communication is impossible when you do not care about what the other person is saying. Insincerity and the "you're wrong/I'm right" attitude eliminates the rapport between two people. Conversations are not something you can "win," and they are not always about finding a right or wrong answer. This is especially true when the conversation is about a difficult or sensitive topic. This is exactly when good communication is needed the most. If you approach others with genuine interest in what they have to say, even if it differs from what you think, effective communication is more likely to occur.

I once worked for a boss who had an ineffective approach to conversation. He would ask a probing question to a subordinate. When the person would be about halfway into an answer, the boss would say "whoa, whoa, whoa" and make a "time out" sign. The subordinate would stop speaking, and the boss would ask another question but again interrupt the reply. This would go on for several cycles without the subordinate ever finishing one answer.

I don't think he meant any disrespect to his employees. However, as a leader, the ultimate test is not what you meant but rather what you communicated. In this case, by continuously interrupting, the boss was extremely rude and disrespectful to his people. It appeared he chose to interrupt simply because he could. As leaders, restraint of your power is sometimes necessary for good communication to exist.

Another important part of communication is an appreciation of when to keep quiet. This is particularly true for leaders because people pay close attention to what you say. There are going to be times when you don't know what you're talking about, and those are really the times to refrain from speaking until you have more information. This principle is demonstrated by the following story:

A hungry mountain lion came out of the hills, attacked a bull, and killed it. As it feasted on its kill, the lion would, from time to time, pause to roar in triumph. A hunter heard the commotion, found the lion, and shot him dead. The moral of the story is: when you're full of bull, keep your mouth shut.

Remember that as a leader you communicate through more than just words. Your actions, body language, inflection, mannerisms, and your behavior all communicate a great deal to your listeners. Words are important, but there is much more to communication than just verbal language.

There is an *I Love Lucy* episode in which Lucy ends up in France charged with counterfeiting. Ricky arrived to help, but there were major communication problems. The sergeant spoke only French, and Lucy spoke only English. However, one of the officers spoke French and German. One of the other prisoners spoke German and Spanish. Ricky, of course, spoke Spanish and English. They formed a communication line and translated French to German to Spanish to English. This very funny scene hits close to home with many organizations. Although we may all be speaking the same language, it may not always appear that way. It is the leader's duty to ensure that messages are communicated effectively.

Even when the leader communicates with great precision, things can still go wrong. In my seminars, I do an exercise in communication where I give one of the members of the class a short paragraph to read. This person in turn is required to pass it on. After four or five people have passed the message down the line, I ask someone to repeat the message. It always comes out terribly distorted.

In the exercise, the first person gets the message in pristine written condition, which is rarely the case in a workplace. Then, over a two-minute period, the message is passed

from person to person. Normally, organizational communications occur over weeks, even months, making the message
even more prone to corruption. This exercise showcases that
even under optimum conditions communication can be
difficult.

The following story shows how communications can
easily go astray:

Delivering a speech at a banquet on the night of
his arrival into a large city, a visiting minister told
several anecdotes he expected to repeat at meetings
the next day. Because he wanted to use the jokes
again, he requested that the reporters omit them from
any accounts they might run in their newspapers. A
cub reporter, in commenting on the speech, ended his
piece with the following: "The minister told a
number of stories that cannot be published."

Church bulletins have even been an amusing source of
misleading communications, as evidenced by the following
actual excerpts:

- Don't let worry kill you – let the church help.

- Remember in prayer the many who are sick of our church
  and community.

- For those who have children and don't know it, we have a
  new nursery.

- This being Easter Sunday, we ask Mrs. Lewis to come
  forward and lay an egg on the altar.

- Thursday, there will be a meeting of the Little Mothers
  Club. All wishing to become little mothers, please see the
  minister in his study.

Communication is invariably going to involve the
occasional disagreement. There are going to be times when

you must debate an issue with others, and there will be times when you, as the leader, will need to mediate an argument between people. There are healthy, constructive ways to debate that promote discussion and evaluation, and there are ways of arguing that evade the issues and usually only end up causing frustration or insult.

You need to be aware of where a disagreement goes from normal dissent to destructive arguing. Discussion allows both sides to be heard freely and without bias. It is where people speak respectfully, rationally, stay on topic, and avoid illogical fallacies that can cloud the issue. This type of debate is productive; it allows both sides of an issue to be discussed and evaluated. When you communicate in this manner, you have a better chance of getting your points across intact and faithfully representing your side. Then, the best choice can be made. Some fallacies to look for and avoid when disagreeing include:

- Attacking the person (put-downs, bringing up the past, etc.) instead of the issue.

- Attempting to discredit the person instead of focusing on the issues.

- Generalizing that may not be representative or relevant.

- Using fear or pity to gain support for an argument.

- Comparing issues or situations that are dissimilar.

- Excluding factors or evidence that may affect the debate.

- Not giving all the options or consequences of a situation.

- Assuming something is false because you do not know it to be true.

- Assuming something is true because it is generally believed to be true.

- Using the "slippery slope" approach where consequences increase from bad to worse. Example: If I let you go home early on Friday, then everyone will want to go home early on Friday. Soon everyone will want all of Friday off, and we'll get nothing done.

- Basing the argument on unrelated or improbable points.

- Attaching moral superiority or goodness to a debater and therefore to his or her argument.

- Using non sequiturs where the conclusion does not follow from the premise. Example: Because Lily types quickly, she must be good at computer programming.

- Arguing that two contradictory points are both true.

- Concluding about the whole of something (a group, situation, etc.) when you have only discussed part(s) of it.

- Using untested or biased evidence.

- Using too-broad or too-narrow definitions.

- Using words or phrases that allow for varying interpretations.

- "Begging the question" when you must assume the truth of the conclusion before you can assume the truth of the premise.

- Attacking arguments that are different from what the other person is actually arguing.

So in regards to communication, what's the answer for the leader? You must communicate clearly, often, and consistently. Constantly seek feedback to see if the message has been sent and if it has been received accurately. Practice active listening so that you truly understand the perspectives of others – never assume that you know what another person thinks before you communicate. Also, you must have a genuine interest in what other people have to say, even if it differs from your own ideas. When you face a disagreement, make sure both sides are using healthy, constructive arguments and avoiding fallacies. Good communication is not always easy, but it is an essential element for smooth operations within your organization.

Chapter Analysis

Keys to Understanding

- Focus a great deal on communicating effectively.

- Show your respect for others by how you communicate with them. This includes how you listen to your workers.

- Remember that listening is perhaps the most important part of communicating.

- As a leader, your words have great power. Choose them wisely and use them gently.

Questions for Reflection

1. In what ways does taking the time for "active listening" impair your ability to get things done? How do you balance the need to listen to people with time constraints?

2. How do you show that you are an active listener?

3. How do you balance the open-door policy with the need for line authority?

4. How do you foster good communication skills?

Chapter 21

Decision Making

When you come to a fork in the road, take it.

–Yogi Berra

The man who insists upon seeing with perfect clearness before he decides, never decides.

–Henri-Frederic Amiel

Most people have worked for bosses who were indecisive. I once worked for one who wanted to study everything to death. No matter how much information he assembled, it never seemed enough for him to make the call. I think if the building caught on fire, he would have formed a steering committee and developed an action plan on how we should go about escaping!

Police officers are called upon to make split-second decisions on a regular basis. Some of these decisions involve life-or-death situations. As part of my job, I have to continually evaluate the decisions that my officers make. I always try to evaluate the decision based upon the information that was available to the officer at the time. Further, I try to decide whether the decision was reasonable against the totality of the circumstances. If it was, I will support the decision, even if it was not the same one that I would have made. It is important for leaders to be empathetic and to remember that there are many different ways to do the job correctly.

In his book *Further Up the Organization,* Robert Townsend makes some interesting observations about the decision-making process:

> There are two kinds of decisions: those that are expensive to change and those that are not. Common decisions – like when to have the cafeteria open for lunch or what brand of pencil to buy – should be made fast. No point in taking three weeks to make a decision that can be made in three seconds and corrected inexpensively later if wrong. The whole organization may be out of business while you oscillate between baby blue and buffalo brown coffee cups.

If you have the luxury of taking time to make an important decision, certainly do so. Use that extra time to research the issue and solicit input from the people impacted. Everyone understands the desire to carefully plan and check a decision. However, people usually can sense when time is up, and they will look to the leader as the one to come forth with a decision. If leaders either cannot or will not do this, their credibility will suffer. Also, many decisions are time sensitive. You will not have an extended time period in which to make your conclusion. Having an indecisive person in a leadership position can have a very adverse impact not only on employee morale but also on the goals of the organization.

To be a good decision maker, you must avoid procrastination. There are some key points to remember in order to bypass this problem. First, you must be aware of your own style of reasoning and thinking. You may require some reflection and meditation to assess your decision-making style. Work with your style to arrive at sound, timely decisions. You may also want to inquire about other's thinking and reasoning processes. How do they differ from your own? Do they give you any new insight or perspectives?

Next, you should set a time and deadline for your decision to be made. This will give you a concrete goal to reach. When it comes to tough decisions, you should ask for the input of others to see if they have found any angles that you may have missed. Make a list of all the various alternatives and include the pros and cons of each. Look at the concrete data available to you. Which alternatives seem more logical and beneficial? You should also evaluate the assumptions that you are making during the decision-making process and determine whether or not these are valid. Finally, make the decision and stick with it.

You should document the decision and the factors that were involved. Why did you make this particular decision? What were your alternatives, and why were they not chosen? After some time, you may want to add the consequences, both positive and negative, that resulted from your decision. This type of documentation will help you to evaluate your decision-making process in the future and help you to become a better, faster, more effective decision maker.

A relative of the indecisive person is the "waffler." In many ways, this person is even harder to deal with than someone who is just plain indecisive. The "waffler" will make a decision but will continually reverse it. I have worked for one of these people only once in my career, and it was an arduous experience. I could never count on anything this person would say, and this, of course, made it difficult to do my job. Sometimes the decision would be changed within a few months, sometimes within a few weeks, and sometimes within a few days. There were even times when the decision would be reversed several minutes after it was made! The "waffler" usually gave no reason to explain why the decision had to be changed. In the rare cases where a reason was given, it was often nonsensical.

It became an organizational joke; we would literally look at our watches and make guesses about when the latest decision would be reversed. I finally developed an effective tactic to handle my "waffler." Whenever he would give me a decision that I thought was good, I would work to implement it with breakneck speed. It wasn't at all uncommon for the "waffler" to come to me with a decision reversal. However, I would be able to tell him that it was too late and that I had already implemented his instructions. Because he had no choice, he would reluctantly accept this.

In cases where he gave me a decision that was poor, I would sit on it and wait for him to change his mind, which he very often would. The techniques I was forced to implement were a bit ridiculous. I am not particularly proud of this type of orchestration, but sometimes, you do what you have to do for the good of the organization.

Consultation and delegation can be vital elements of the decision-making process. As a leader, you are going to have to determine when you will decide alone and when you will collaborate with others. Making decisions collaboratively is often beneficial because it can include the people involved, and it allows for more than one perspective on the issue. However, there will be times when this is neither possible nor desirable. If the decision must be made quickly or if you alone will be held accountable, you will probably have to decide on your own.

On occasion, you may have to reverse your decision; it happens. However, keep these occurrences to a minimum. Make sure you have justifiable reasons and then explain to the appropriate people *why* you had to change the decision. If you have a rational reason for changing course, people will accept it, and your reputation will be enhanced. Remember that although you should acquire information and get input prior to making most decisions, too much intellectualizing can paralyze the decision-making process, the proverbial "paralysis by analysis."

Planning for Decision Making

When making a decision, whether it is involves a problem you face or a task you want completed, it is sometimes helpful to make a written plan of how you are going to proceed. Here are some steps to help you during the decision-making process:

✓ First, identify the goal you want accomplished or the problem you want resolved.

✓ List any possible problems that may arise. Think of possible solutions to these problems.

✓ Decide who will be involved. This includes employees working on the task and other departments or organizations.

✓ Determine what resources you will need, from equipment and training to funding.

✓ Create a timeline for when your decisions will be carried out and set deadlines for goal completion.

✓ Determine how you will evaluate the decision in light of what happens.

◊

If no one ever took risks, Michelangelo would have painted the Sistine floor.
—Neil Simon

◊

Chapter Analysis

Keys to Understanding

- After gathering as much information as is reasonable, be decisive.

- Indecisive people in leadership positions adversely affect organizational morale.

- Don't change your decision unless there is an extraordinary change in circumstances.

- If a decision changes, whenever possible, communicate the reasons behind that change.

Questions for Reflection

1. Does your organization have a procedure or formal process for decision making?

2. What different decision models does your organization use? Which do you use?

3. Have you been subject to "paralysis by analysis"? What part does intuition play in the decision process?

4. How and when do you involve others in decision making?

Chapter 22

Change

If you want to make enemies, try to change something.

–Woodrow Wilson

Change has no constituency.

–Machiavelli

Change is inevitable. It occurs continually and is one of the most stressful events for organizations. There are many factors, such as fear or insecurity, which create uneasiness regarding change. Both leaders and employees are prone to resist changes. Sometimes, people view it as a sign that their current work is not good enough, and they become defensive about ways to improve. Good leaders recognize this and do everything they can to ease the impact surrounding organizational change.

There are two types of change for an organization, internally-imposed change and externally-imposed change. Leaders need to understand that there will be situations brought about by external sources, and there may be limits to how much control they have on these situations. Their only option may be a reactive posture. Internally-imposed changes offer a better opportunity to shape the organization's future in a proactive way. The one constant is that change is a guaranteed occurrence within any organization. Good leaders have the ability to adapt and also to lead others through the stressful process of adaptation. Ideally, leaders do not just react; they proact. It is their job to make the workplace one in which change is viewed positively.

Leaders who are new to an organization, or to a particular division, must remember that any changes they make may suggest an implicit criticism of the existing structure. This is going to occur despite how the reason for change is framed. Although you cannot remain stagnant just to avoid offending anyone, you must be sensitive to people's concerns. Change is difficult for most people, even if the change is perceived as positive. If it is viewed negatively, there is even more potential for resistance. You can take the brute-force approach and force changes. However, good leaders understand that in order to create a lasting effect, change must be inspired. Remember the Eisenhower string? Leaders can help their people to assimilate in several ways.

First, whether you are new to the job or implementing change in your current position, you should involve the people affected by the situation. Begin by explaining why you perceive the change to be necessary. It is always a good idea to get multiple perspectives before considering new directions. Also, this will give your employees a sense of empowerment and involvement, which will ease the pressures of changing. Secondly, whenever possible, time should be allotted in the process to allow people to acclimate fully to the change. People will be less anxious if they feel that they have had enough time to prepare for a new challenge. Prior to the change, the organization's approach should be communicated in writing. Finally, if additional training is required, this training should be conducted prior to the implementation of the change. After the implementation, feedback should be solicited. It is possible that some midcourse corrections will be warranted.

Even if these steps are followed, change will still be a challenge. However, it may be accepted more easily and in a shorter amount of time. People will understand the need for the change, they will have had an opportunity for input, and they will have the confidence that they can successfully deal with the new situation.

◊

Every leader, to be effective, must simultaneously adhere to the symbols of change and revision and the symbols of tradition and stability.

–Alfred Whitehead

◊

Chapter Analysis

Keys to Understanding

- Even positive change can be stressful for an organization.
- Include impacted people in the pre-change planning session.
- Whenever possible, implement change gradually.
- Seek out feedback after you implement change.

Questions for Reflection

1. What steps have you taken to improve your organization's acceptance of change? What is your reaction to change?

2. How does considering the stress that will result from a particular decision influence your decisions?

3. In what ways do your employees have control over their environment?

4. How is the ability to adapt to change built into the employee-hiring evaluation process? What about the employee-review process?

Chapter 22 Worksheet: Evaluating Change

Yes No

☐ ☐ 1. Employees were involved in determining the need for change and how to meet that need.

☐ ☐ 2. Employees were "in the know" in regards to the market, clients, company policy, etc. so that they could recognize the need for changes.

☐ ☐ 3. Employees were involved in the planning process prior to the change.

☐ ☐ 4. Any objections employees might have had were considered during the planning stage.

☐ ☐ 5. The intended results of the change were clearly communicated.

☐ ☐ 6. The change was explained to all who would be affected by it; they knew what would be involved in the present and in the future.

☐ ☐ 7. A specific plan for implementing change was created.

☐ ☐ 8. People were allowed to voice ideas and concerns in a constructive manner.

☐ ☐ 9. All leaders demonstrated a positive attitude, which communicated that they believed in the success of the change.

☐ ☐ 10. A variety of feedback was gathered after the change.

☐ ☐ 11. Any needed adjustments were recognized and implemented following the change.

** You should have answered "yes" to at least eight of these questions. Next time you implement change, think about the areas you missed and come up with new ideas to help change occur more smoothly and easily.

Chapter 23

Competing Concerns

A President's hardest task is not to do what is right but to know what is right.

–Lyndon Johnson

The phrase "balancing competing concerns" sums up the career of almost every executive. A leader is constantly confronted with clashing issues. Sometimes these issues are conflicting goals; sometimes they are conflicting people or groups of people.

Leaders must take in as much information as possible and make the choice that best accomplishes the organization's mission. A good vision statement is vital when attempting to balance different issues and problematic situations. Sometimes, the proper course of action will become clear simply by consulting the corporate vision statement.

Many conflicts between competing concerns can be resolved at the planning phase. Leaders should continually be engaged in short-term and long-term planning. Plans should be ambitious, thorough, flexible, and realistic, and goals should be specific and achievable. They must take into account competing concerns, and they must prioritize tasks. Once you know what the top priorities are, situations that jeopardize them can be more effectively assessed. It is also helpful to think of potential obstacles while still in the planning phase. You should analyze what problems may arise while working toward your goal and think about possible solutions to these issues.

Leaders should require their people to plan properly as well. When Peter Uberroth was the director of the planning effort for the 1984 Olympics, he had a sign on his desk that read: "Lack of planning on your part, does not constitute a crisis on my part."

Good leaders rely on planning to help balance competing concerns. They also effectively react to changing conditions and work to identify emerging issues. It is more difficult to make a good decision when a situation takes you by surprise, so good plans always try to include several alternative scenarios.

Sometimes you will find that the competing concerns are between people or groups of people. The leader's job in such a situation is to negotiate between the disputing factions. There may be many different views on one issue, and it may seem difficult to maintain cohesion in your organization at these times. The key is to rise to the occasion and serve as an impartial mediator in such disputes. Whether you are hearing a conflict between two people or many, you must bring people together to communicate on the issues, discuss them, and focus on possible solutions. You should always seek out a mutually acceptable conclusion. If you don't appear to be fair in these situations or if you display favoritism, your integrity and reputation will be hurt. People will not want to come to you with disputes. Effective leaders possess mediation skills, and they can negotiate between conflicting concerns and people, bringing both parties together in rational, cooperative discussions.

Chapter Analysis

Keys to Understanding

- Effective leaders balance competing concerns in a way that is fair and equitable.

- When in doubt, examine the organization's vision or mission statement. Favor the path that most directly aligns with the statement.

- Leaders should possess good mediation skills so that they can effectively negotiate between disagreeing factions.

Questions for Reflection

1. Have you ever had to balance competing concerns? How did you resolve the situation?

2. Have you had training in mediation skills? If so, how did it affect your leadership? If not, how would it affect your leadership?

3. How do you do your planning? Is it within or outside of the organization's formal planning process? How is it documented?

4. How do you build flexibility into your plans? Do you run a "what if...then" series of scenarios? Do you identify the major elements that are likely to change? Do you run through a plan to determine which factors are the most disruptive if they change?

When You Don't Know

*If man evolved from monkeys and apes, why do we
still have monkeys and apes?*

–George Carlin

Despite a leader's best efforts to continually stay
informed and educated, there will be many times where the
right answer or right way to proceed is unknown. Nobody
expects a leader to know everything all the time. As a leader,
however, the responsibility to act under such circumstances
belongs to you. At this point, there are two basic options. You
can admit it and seek out the appropriate information or you
can attempt to bluff your way through.

Although there are certainly leaders who will disagree
with me, I almost always select the first option. I think it is
preferable to admit when you don't know the answer. Of
course people want a confident and able leader. A worker
wants to feel that if they need guidance or help, they can
always turn to their boss to find answers that they do not have.

However, I do not think that people expect their
leaders to have all the answers. In fact, no one appreciates a
"know it all," even at the managerial level. Furthermore,
admitting that you do not know the answer humbles you and
lets your employees see that you are human as well. People
want integrity from their leaders. They are more loyal and
productive when they believe in the moral character of their
leader. An integral part of demonstrating integrity is being

honest, even if it means showing that you do not know something.

As a leader, you should maintain some degree of humility. Although you do not want to be meek and controllable, you also do not want to be overbearing and arrogant. It is acceptable to have pride in your work and your accomplishments, but there is a needed balance. You are not going to know everything, and you are not always going to be right. Being humble means that you acknowledge this human frailty and allow the input and help of others when needed. Humility will also allow you to face suggestions gracefully when you do ask for help. If people are continually faced with arrogance each time they try to help, they will eventually stop sharing their ideas and creativity.

Along these same lines, I encourage others to admit when they are wrong. Most people do not like to do this, and leaders are no exception. The following story illustrates the type of stubborn behavior some employees have to deal with from their leaders:

There was a man who believed he was dead. Much to the dismay of his family and friends, they were unable to convince him that he was in fact alive. Out of desperation, they made an appointment for him to see a psychiatrist. The proficient doctor spent many painstaking hours with the client trying to convince him that he was alive. He used every angle he could think of, but nothing seemed to work. Finally, the doctor ran across one final approach. He spent a few sessions with the man talking about the physical impossibility of dead people bleeding. After hours of tedious convincing, the patient relented. "So you do agree that a dead person can't bleed?" asked the psychiatrist. "Yes, I do," the patient replied. With a sigh of relief, the doctor pulled out a pin and pricked the

man's finger. Out came a squirt of blood. "Now,"
the doctor asked, "What does that show you?"
Pausing briefly, the man got a startled look on his face
and replied, "I would have never thought it so...dead
men do bleed."

Everyone probably has a similar story about a boss
who just could not admit to being wrong. As a leader, you
have a responsibility to set aside your ego and admit if you
have made a mistake or have been wrong. This allows the
problem to be solved and helps everyone to move on as quickly
as possible. Admitting error is difficult, especially when you
are the leader and feel as though you are held to a higher
standard. However, not acknowledging a mistake and
postponing any needed corrections may cost your organization, in tangible (money) or intangible (time, morale) ways.
This is certainly not what a good leader is charged to do. In
the long run, you will attain a higher level of respect if you
take full responsibility for your actions and decisions.

I once worked for a boss who made all the wrong
moves when he was uncertain about an issue. Of course, to
hear him tell it, there was nothing he didn't know! He
would never admit he was wrong, even though he was
repeatedly. Whenever in doubt, he would try to bluff his way
through. Worse yet, when he would finally ask a question and
someone would answer it, he would say, "I know that." Of
course, we were tempted to ask him why he had asked the
question at all if he already knew the answer. This type of
boss can alienate people quickly with such arrogant behavior.

Regardless of what comes your way as a leader, work
the problem out logically to come to a solution. The fact that
you did not have an immediate answer is not a big deal. What's
important is that you effectively handled the issue. Now, if as a
leader you *never* seem to know the answer or how to effectively

proceed, that is another situation entirely. At that point, perhaps another line of work is in order!

If you begin to recognize a pattern in the types of areas that challenge you, this is a good time to identify a weakness and work to strengthen it. Initial lack of knowledge is acceptable but remaining ignorant to recognized problems is not. You may find that you have difficulty making decisions in a particular field because you lack the expertise to do so. Identify these areas and strive to become better educated in these subjects. This will make you a more effective leader.

Chapter Analysis

Keys to Understanding

- As a leader, it's okay to show your human side. Part of this is admitting that you don't know the answer to everything.

- As a general rule, do not bluff to subordinates.

- If you identify a particular area in which your knowledge is weak, work to improve it!

Questions for Reflection

1. When is it acceptable, or even desirable, to "bluff" subordinates?

2. What are the limits to admitting that you do not know the answer?

3. At what point do leaders face the prospect that they are deficient in skills in an area that is critical to their leadership? What should these people do about it?

Chapter 25

Innovation

Great innovations should not be forced on slender majorities.

–Thomas Jefferson

In *A Whack on the Side of the Head,* Roger Von Oech recounts the story of how the keys on a typewriter came to be ordered in the familiar but inefficient "QWERTY" fashion:

> Back in the 1870's, Sholes and Company, the leading manufacturer of typewriters at the time, received many complaints from users about the typewriter keys sticking together if the operator went too quickly. In response, top management asked its engineers to figure out a way to prevent this from happening. The engineers discussed the problem for awhile until they concluded that the answer was to have a fairly inefficient keyboard configuration. Engineers designed a keyboard so that the weaker fingers would be required to hit some of the more common keys. This approach was used to solve the "problem." Since that solution was reached, typewriter and word processing technology has advanced significantly. There are now typewriters that can go much faster than any human operator can type. The problem is that the "QWERTY" configuration continues to be used even though there are faster configurations available. Once a rule is established, it is very difficult to eliminate it even if the original reason for its generation has gone away.

Leaders should be innovators, and they should always be on the lookout for "QWERTY" situations occurring in their operations. Innovation, like change, is difficult to implement. It is better inspired than imposed. Fortunately for leaders, if they have hired good people, this will not be a problem. Innovative ideas will continually emanate from below. It becomes the leader's job to ensure that innovative ideas are not met with resistance.

Some classic, innovation-killing phrases are:

- Yes, but we've always done it this way.

- It's not in the budget.

- If it ain't broke, don't fix it.

- We already tried that.

You can reject ideas or set guidelines, and many times it will be appropriate to do so, just proceed with caution. Your words have more power than you realize; it is easy to kill a new idea in its infancy with a careless, off-handed comment. New ideas are like any newborn form of life. They are weak at first and must be nurtured until they are strong enough to survive on their own. Leaders should treat promising new ideas with respect, and if they are to be discarded, it should be done gently. One never knows – the idea that is not right today may be perfect tomorrow or next week.

You want to create an environment where people are encouraged to come to you with new thoughts or approaches. If you ignore people's feelings, they may not want to offer their thoughts in the future. In treating sincere suggestions carelessly, you may inadvertently drain your office of the creative and innovative thinking that precedes beneficial change. An environment devoid of freethinking is never good for the long-term health of any organization.

Chapter Analysis

Keys to Understanding

- Seek innovation from those who report to you.

- Remember that sometimes the best time to fix something is when it's not broken.

- When you reject new ideas, do so with tact and gentleness.

Questions for Reflection

1. Do you stifle or encourage innovation? How many significant improvements have you shepherded in the last year?

2. How does the administration of a top-down idea differ from the process for a bottom-up idea?

3. How does "that requires more study" and other such phrases end up being used as roadblocks to innovation?

Chapter
26

Consistency

It is not best to swap horses while crossing the river.

–Abraham Lincoln

If workers have a common complaint, it is lack of consistency on the part of management. People want the same action to be taken each and every time the same issue occurs. First and foremost, they want consistency because they perceive it as the fair way of doing things. Nobody likes favoritism or special treatment. They want to see that management imposes an even and fair hand in comparable situations. This means giving out rewards and punishment in a consistent manner. People also want management's actions to be predictable and consistent. Workers want to know what will happen to them in given circumstances, and they want to be able to predict this based on what occurred in the past.

Leaders need to understand employees' desire for consistency. However, it is a very difficult thing to achieve for a variety of reasons. First, management usually has access to a greater amount of information about the specifics of an individual situation. This is particularly true in confidential personnel matters. Two situations may appear alike to the worker but, in fact, may be drastically different.

This type of misunderstanding most commonly comes into play in disciplinary cases. Two employees, at different times, engage in the same misconduct. The penalties may be quite different, based on such things as the employee's seniority, aggravating/mitigating factors, work history, and past record of discipline. To workers viewing the situation, it may appear that the two situations are similar and that the penalties should be equal. This is where the question of fairness and consistency is often raised.

In addition, times and circumstances do change. No organization is going to do things the same way forever, so there will be changes along the way in what is emphasized and prioritized. When actions taken by management appear in contradiction to established norms, the issue of consistency with past practice is brought forward as an issue.

The necessity for different actions taken in similar cases is shown in the following story:

When Harry was a young boy in Louisiana, he was always getting into trouble. One morning, while waiting for the school bus, he pushed the outhouse into the bayou and went off to school as if nothing had happened. When he returned, his father was waiting for him. He said, "Son, did you push the outhouse into the bayou?" "Yes, father," said Harry, "like George Washington, I cannot tell a lie." Harry's father took off his belt and said, "All right, son, bend over. I'm going to have to whip you." Harry tried to explain that Mr. Washington had not spanked George when he had admitted to chopping down the cherry tree. "Yes, son," said Harry's father, "but George's father wasn't in the tree."

In Harry's mind, his situation was no different than what had happened to George Washington. Therefore, he felt that he should receive the same penalty. His father explained the not-so-subtle differences between the situations. Although Harry might not have liked this "inconsistency," at least he understood his father's reasoning.

As a leader, you should strive for consistency when handling matters that are precisely the same. If you are going to change what you do, explain to people why extenuating circumstances make the situations unique. When you articulate rational reasons, people will be much more inclined to understand. This in turn creates less friction among management and employees and reduces the perception of inconsistent practices. You may not always be able to explain your decisions because of confidential or sensitive information. However, if you have built a reputation for fairness and consistency, you will likely retain the support of your staff.

Chapter Analysis

Keys to Understanding

- Be consistent in your actions unless there are good reasons for deviating from past practice.

- Whenever possible, divulge the reasons for why you chose to deviate from standard procedure.

Questions for Reflection

1. Do you feel an obligation to explain your actions to your subordinates? How does this encourage or discourage a feeling of consistency?

2. Do you feel that your organization is consistent in policy and procedures?

3. At what point do exacting policy and procedures stifle management discretion?

Chapter
27

Leadership Approaches

*A leader has two important characteristics; first, he is going somewhere-
second, he is able to persuade other people to go with him.*

–Maximilien Robespierre

There are many different approaches to leadership.
Each leader has their individual personality and style that will
affect how they manage their workers. However, good leaders
also take into account the situation, people, and organization
when deciding how they will approach the leadership role.
Simply using whatever style comes easiest for you is not always
going to produce the best results.

Some people are "hands-off" managers and others are
"hands-on" leaders. Hands-on management sometimes turns
into "micromanagement" where the boss must have control
over virtually everything. Neither type is right or wrong, certain
employees need certain things. Some need a great deal of
structure and want to be guided every step of the way. Others
resent this and want a more hands-off approach where they are
allowed more individual liberty in their work. It is important to
assess each employee for what they need from management,
something that takes time. If you give employees the type of
leadership they need rather than what comes naturally to you,
they will be much more productive and happy.

Authorities such as Paul Hersey and Ken Blanchard
have articulated the concept of situational leadership. The
Hersey and Blanchard model views the leadership approach in
relation to the situation and group involved. The basic notion

is that leaders should have a toolbox filled with different approaches and resources for effective leadership. Depending on what factors are present in the situation and who is being led, the leader selects the style of leadership that will most likely yield the best results. By choosing the appropriate approach based on these criteria, the leaders can ensure a higher probability for success and development of their people.

For example, if a leader in law enforcement is confronted with a hostage situation, that person will probably adopt an autocratic style of leadership with the recovery forces. This is simply because that type of situation requires orders to be given and followed immediately. There is no time to break into small groups and make lists on a flip chart. The situation has dictated the appropriate style of leadership.

The personalities of the people being led are also a key factor in which style a leader should select. Their ability and skill level must be assessed to determine what will help them to succeed. For example, if there is a well-trained, experienced, and motivated work group, the leader will probably allow them a great deal of freedom and autonomy. On the other hand, if it is a new group that has not shown much in the way of performance or motivation, the leader may be inclined to select a more authoritative and watchful style of leadership. Again, the style is dictated in part by the readiness and willingness of those being led.

It is difficult to be a situational leader. It forces you to constantly evaluate the present situation, including the skills and motivations of those working for you. In addition, everyone has a style that comes most naturally. Often, the leadership style most suited to the situation and people is not the style with which the leader personally feels most comfortable.

When I first entered law enforcement employment 20 years ago, the different bosses in my organization would rotate around on a regular basis. Each had an individual style, and it was up to us as officers to adapt to their styles, not the other way around. This made it easy for the bosses, as they just had to do what came naturally. The employees were the ones who had to alter their style to fit the boss.

Although there are still some leaders like this, the concept of situational leadership has taken hold. Now leaders are being asked to adapt, rather than the employees. It is much easier for one person to change and adapt to the work group rather than the group adapting to one person. I strongly believe in situational leadership. It is not easy, but leadership is not always supposed to be easy. It takes a lot of desire and practice to become a good situational leader, but I think that the results are well worth the dedication it requires.

Another approach to leadership is described in Tannenbaum and Schmidt's decision-making model. It is a continuum that looks at how a leader exerts control over a group in order to manage them. Chris Loynes outlines the six positions of this model in the 1993-94 *Expedition Planners Handbook and Directory*.

Tannenbaum and Schmidt's decision-making model:

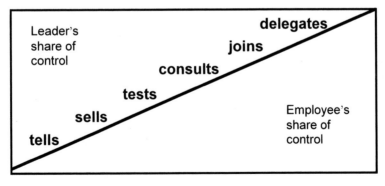

Degree of employee involvement in decision making

1. Tells

Leaders make decisions based on their own evaluation. They decide what action will occur and then tell the group. They do not give explanations, and employees are not involved in the process.

2. Sells

Leaders again make the decision but give the group reasons for what they decided.

3. Tests

Leaders evaluate the situation and offer a solution along with reasons. Before making a final decision, leaders allow questions and discussion from the group.

4. Consults

Leaders present the situation and its background and ask for ideas on solutions. Leaders then make the decision.

5. Joins

Leaders present the problem and then begin a discussion with the group. The decision is made jointly by the group and the leaders.

6. Delegates

Leaders or members of the group present the situation. The group is responsible for coming to a decision about what actions need to be taken. Leaders may participate in the discussion, and they support the decision once it is made.

From approach one to six, the leader is gradually sharing more control with employees. I would like to add a seventh position to this model. Following delegation, there is an additional phase, which is best described as "supervision." This phase is concerned with the level of follow-up and review that a leader exercises over tasks. If a leader does not supervise a delegated task, that is in a sense abdication of the leadership role. On the other hand, if a leader is "micromanaging" every step of the task, that is not true delegation.

Leaders must find the appropriate balance between abdication and "micromanagement," just as a balance between "telling" and "delegation" must be found. The extreme ends of the leadership continuum are rarely appropriate in most organizations. The leader must go back to the situational analysis of the problem. You determine the nature of the issue and the people involved to decide which phase you will initiate to solve a problem or confront a task. If you are flexible enough to adjust your management style to whatever situation and group you encounter, you will likely lead your organization wisely and successfully.

Chapter Analysis

Keys to Understanding

- Situational leadership recognizes that the best style of leadership may vary depending on the situation and the people involved.

- Situational leadership is simple in concept but complex in application.

- Only those who really want to be situational leaders should engage in this approach.

Questions for Reflection

1. How is situational leadership different from situational ethics? Compare and contrast the two.

2. Where are you along the continuum of leadership styles? How does your style compare to the operative or normative model in your organization?

3. How do you communicate your style of leadership and its boundaries?

Chapter 28

Proper Equipment

*So much of what we call management consists of
making it difficult for people to work.*

—Peter Drucker

One of the most fundamental aspects of being a leader is ensuring that your people have appropriate tools to do their jobs. This seems elementary, but it is an area that leaders sometimes forget about. I see the leader's role as similar to that of an offensive lineman in football. You need to block in order to ensure that your people are able to get the football (resources they need). Once the running backs (employees) have obtained the necessary resources, they proceed down the field (doing their jobs). The offensive lineman (the leader) then identifies obstacles and moves them out of the way, so that the running backs can score a touchdown (accomplish the mission).

Leaders need to proactively work to identify what resources and equipment their people need. This seems simple since employees will be more than happy to tell you what they need; all you have to do is ask. There are some leaders who either don't think to ask or don't care to ask. Then there are some who feel that the returns on investment can be maximized by minimizing expenditures on equipment. The other issue that sometimes comes up is the propensity of people to request caviar when a turkey sandwich would do. A leader must realize a balance between needs and desires.

Proper tools and equipment are important to employees so that they can do their jobs properly, but there is another component to this equation. People want to feel needed and respected. Management shows concern for people when equipment needs are taken care of promptly. People will know that you value their time and efforts because you are actively working to ensure that they can proceed uninterrupted.

There is the issue of cost justifying equipment. A wise leader looks for cost and return on investment. The constraints of the organization's financial plan are a good place to start. The leader should seek a return that exceeds the cost of capital. In the end, there are many quantitative and qualitative factors.

Law enforcement officers possess a lot of equipment. This includes a car, a handgun, handcuffs, a radio, report forms, and other items. All workers have their "tools of the trade." It is a leader's job to ensure that the people are properly equipped. Other than the hardware that your employees require, they also need proper training and on-going education to succeed. Obviously, you will not excel if you lack the knowledge or skills required to do a job. With the rapidity of change, leaders must make sure that their workers are receiving adequate training.

Chapter Analysis

Keys to Understanding

- Ensure that your people are properly equipped. This includes training, education, and equipment.

- Management can show concern for people by providing the necessary tools for effective production.

Questions for Reflection

1. At what point do "tools" become "toys" – can employees have too much technology? Is so, how is the distinction and decision made? How do you evaluate costs versus payback?

2. How do you assess what tools and training are required?

Chapter
29

Promotions

*It is a fine thing to have ability, but the ability to discover
ability in others is the true test.*

−Elbert Hubbard

Promotions within your organization make statements
so loudly that almost every other action you take as a leader
can be drowned out. People see who gets promoted, and they
make a variety of judgments accordingly. This process is
called observational learning, and it is the "hidden" process
that always impacts leadership decisions. If the person
promoted is intelligent, hardworking, capable, and honest,
then workers will believe that these are the traits that the
organization values. In turn, those who also wish to be
promoted will tend to emulate these traits.

On the other hand, if the person promoted is perceived to be deceitful, lazy, or incompetent, other employees
may not be motivated to be any other way themselves.
Although their internal self-regulation may keep them from
sinking to this level, they may not be enthused about the
organization in which they work. High turnover and low
morale invariably occurs when employees do not believe in
the integrity of their organization or leaders.

Promotions should be undertaken with great serious-
ness. Although you may have a mission and value statement
posted on the wall, this means nothing if your promotions are
in contradiction to the mission and values. As was mentioned

earlier, people will sometimes believe what you say, but they will almost always believe what you do.

The promotional process in law enforcement is very competitive but also very systemized and regimented. There is usually at least a written test and an oral examination. Ultimately, a promotional list is developed. Most agencies have a "rule of three," which allows the chief executive to choose any candidate among those who scored in the top three. This allows some flexibility, as there are times when certain people who are good test takers come out high on the list. However, this does not automatically mean that these are the best people for the promotion.

The problem in the private sector is that promotions may or may not be subject to any system. In some industries, the "time-and-grade" system still exists, where promotions are based almost exclusively on seniority. In other companies, the process seems to depend on the whims of management. Both of these approaches can lead to apathy, since promotions may have little correlation to performance. In the most enlightened organizations, promotions are based upon a competitive system, with clearly defined job requirements. In these companies, candidates for open positions are sought from within the company before positions are advertised outside.

To the greatest degree possible, any promotional list should be looked at as a guideline. Ultimately, leaders must ensure that the person promoted is the person who is modeling the core values of the organization. Otherwise, there would be a contradiction between the organization's words and its actions. Other employees will certainly recognize this and react accordingly, either with anger or lack of motivation.

Characteristics of Outstanding Workers

Here is a list of characteristics you should look for in an employee before promoting:

✓ Attitude of enthusiasm and "can-do" mentality

✓ Builds esprit de corps

✓ Team player who contributes and compromises

✓ Dependable, reliable, works to potential

✓ Innovative, recognizes opportunity, thinks imaginatively

✓ Has the training, experience, and aptitude to be successful at the next level

✓ Has the desire to be promoted

Chapter Analysis

Keys to Understanding

- Take decisions regarding promotions very seriously.
- Who you choose to promote speaks volumes about what you really feel is important.

Questions for Reflection

1. What is your approach to promotions? Are they 1) organization centered: used as a method of retention, a method of strengthening the organization, or 2) employee based: given on a merit or seniority basis?

2. How do you evaluate the candidate to ensure that the person will be successful at the next level? Do you use tests, interviews, projects, or other means?

3. How do you evaluate the core values of the organization vis-à-vis the demonstrated values of a candidate for promotion?

Dissent vs. Dissension

When two men in business always agree, one of them is unnecessary.

–William Wrigley, Jr.

Like other presidents, William Howard Taft had to endure his share of abuse. One night at the dinner table, his youngest boy made a disrespectful remark to him. There was a sudden hush. Taft looked thoughtful. "Well," said Mrs. Taft to her husband, "aren't you going to punish him?" Taft said, "If the remark was addressed to me as his father, he certainly will be punished. However, if he addressed it to the President of the United States, that is his constitutional privilege."

Smart leaders allow their close advisors to criticize them to a point. Healthy dissent is an important part of making decisions and running an organization. It can help to cover your blind spots as a leader. If you are not open to criticism, you will never improve as a leader or help your organization succeed.

Don't kill the messenger. Whether it is bad news or a criticism of the boss's style, the messenger should not be punished, as long as the dissent does not turn into dissension. In my mind, dissent is when the person still supports the boss and the organization despite a difference in point of view. Dissension is when the differences erupt to the point that the person no longer supports the boss and the organization.

This can occur when the boss is not willing to hear any feedback from employees. They may become resentful that they cannot voice their opinions and have no control over their environment. It can also occur when every suggestion or opinion is ignored. If people have legitimate concerns about their jobs or how to perform them, you must be at least willing to hear them out on the matter. While obviously you will not act on every concern raised by an employee, you should at least consider them and determine when action is necessary.

Many years ago, I arrived into an executive position in an organization. I still remember my first staff meeting where I discussed my expectations. I explained my version of the "kill the messenger theory," and I told them I would never "kill" the messenger. What I would do however is deal harshly with people who neglected to deliver important messages when they should have. They took me at my word and always gave me reports, even if they were unpleasant, and I kept my word and never punished someone who conveyed the message. Even better, no one refused to bring me necessary information. Everyone knew it was not only desired, it was required.

In my case, employees understood the priorities. In some environments, however, the never kill the messenger system may not initially meet with success. The problem is that often employees will resist being forthcoming out of fear or from peer pressure. Dealing with such situations can be challenging because no matter how much you try and convince them, employees generally perceive a wide divide between you and them. It may take a lot of time and patience for that divide to be bridged, particularly if you are attempting to change an established pattern of behavior.

Chapter Analysis

Keys to Understanding

- Take your ego out of the equation as a leader and encourage healthy dissent.
- Healthy dissent gives you new insights and perspectives that you may not have thought of otherwise.
- Don't punish the messenger just because you don't like the news.
- Do not allow dissent to evolve into dissension.

Questions for Reflection

1. How do you tell when dissent becomes dissension?
2. How does a leader preserve the integrity and authority of leadership when dissent is present?
3. How do you let employees know that you are open to feedback and ideas, even if they differ from your own?

Chapter 30 Worksheet:
Your Conflict-Resolution Skills

Yes No

☐ ☐   1.   I engage in active listening, giving the person my full attention and making eye contact.

☐ ☐   2.   I do not interrupt; I let the person finish speaking before I begin.

☐ ☐   3.   I ask questions and paraphrase to make sure that I understand what was said.

☐ ☐   4.   If I disagree, I tell the person and explain why.

☐ ☐   5.   If someone disagrees with my idea, I listen. I do not become defensive or punish the person.

☐ ☐   6.   I recognize that the person has the right to his or her opinion, even if I disagree with it.

☐ ☐   7.   I focus attention on solving the problem, not arguing or bringing up the past.

☐ ☐   8.   I maintain my calm and discuss the situation rationally, no name-calling or put-downs.

☐ ☐   9.   I distinguish between condemning the idea and attacking the person.

☐ ☐   10. If I feel that I cannot control my anger, I step back and take a break. I wait until I have calmed down to discuss the problem again.

☐ ☐   11. When I am wrong, I admit it and take responsibility; I do not try to cover my error or blame others.

** You should have answered yes to at least eight of these questions. If you did not, you need to think about the ways that you can improve your conflict-resolution skills.

Concern For People

Each of the three components in this book (common sense, logic, and concern for people) is important. It is necessary for a leader to perform well in each area and to successfully blend the components in a seamless manner. However, if forced to state which area was most crucial to success, I would say concern for people. This is true because a sincere feeling and concern for people can compensate for a lot of weaknesses in the other two areas. Leadership is first and foremost about dealing with people.

The most valuable quality a leader can possess is good interpersonal skills. Workers are probably the most important components of a business, and bosses affect the attitudes of their employees. When leaders cannot communicate with workers, the organization will experience low morale, a lack of loyalty or dedication from employees, and a high turnover rate. In essence, the attitude of the leader toward people affects the productivity and success of an organization.

This section covers twenty important areas for leaders to address as they approach leadership challenges. People are the most important resources for leaders. Leaders would do well to remember this in every action they take. No organization will thrive without the efforts and dedication of its workers. Similarly, no leader will succeed without the respect and support of their people.

Chapter
31

Integrity

The person who is slowest in making a promise is most faithful in its performance.

−Jean-Jacques Rousseau

The straight and narrow path would be wider if more people used it.

−Kay Ingram

Kouzes and Posner have done extensive survey work in attempting to determine what people want most in their leaders. They found that, among other things, people wanted their leader to be intelligent, fair, competent, and inspiring. The integrity and ethics of leaders have become increasingly important issues. To get workers to be productive and loyal, they must have faith in their leader as a morally virtuous person.

One aspect of integrity is honesty. Leaders should be honest for a variety of reasons. First, it is simply the right thing to do. Morally and ethically speaking, one should be honest in dealings with other people. Second, presumably, one wants employees to be honest. How can you expect this behavior if you do not model it yourself? Also, your level of honesty has direct impact on how people perceive you in other important areas, such as trust, credibility, and dependability.

Even people who are naturally honest sometimes have difficulty with this issue in the workplace. It is not easy to confront someone in a brutally honest fashion; it is not easy to criticize people in a straightforward manner; it is not easy to deal with sensitive matters in direct terms. However, good leaders make every effort to be honest with people at all times. Although difficult, this is what people really want from a leader; they want honesty with empathy. How you deliver the truth is as important as the truth itself. You should be as kind and respectful as you can when delivering bad news; it will help others accept the information more easily.

Then there is the issue of whether or not every truth needs to be communicated. If the truth will not enhance a situation, it may be better left unsaid. For example, if a secretary is a marginal but satisfactory performer and has no chance for promotion, is it necessary to disclose that fact when it is obvious that this person is performing at his or her highest skill level and is happy in the position? Obviously, it makes no sense to use the truth when nothing is to be gained. Truth shouldn't be delivered where it is brutal or harmful.

People today are looking for more than just money out of their jobs. They are seeking out a higher meaning in their lives, both professionally and personally. They want inspiration and fulfillment from their work. In evaluating their lives, they look to their own and their companies' morals and ethics. This includes company policies regarding themselves, other workers, and the society at large. They are also looking closely at the character of their leader.

The reason that this is so important is that it is directly tied to employee retention. The bottom line is that people want an ethical leader. To get loyalty from employees, they must see concern for themselves and others, fairness, honesty, and good moral values from their companies and leaders. For workers, the leaders are the personification of the company. If they see you emulating these virtues, they will have better feelings for the company and will therefore be more loyal. When employees realize that these essentials are missing from their workplace, turnover will increase. Most people do not want to compromise their own integrity by working for a company that does not maintain high values.

Therefore, leaders must create a workplace that employees feel good about from a moral view. You must think about the impact that any action will have on your staff, your company, and society. First, you must define what integrity means to your company. As an organization, create an outline of your most important values. Look to your vision statement and create a code of ethics that will help guide you. Discuss how these values apply to day-to-day operations, how they could be compromised, and how to deal with such situations. Employees should feel comfortable enough to raise concerns they have about ethical problems in their jobs or in the company as a whole.

Once you have defined your values, make sure that you are applying them consistently in every aspect of your organization. Again, you must lead by example. No one is going to believe you are ethical simply by what you say on the subject. Your actions must parallel your words. And remember that it is in the little things that a moral code is demonstrated. If you ignore small ethical transgressions, you are sending a message that, despite your announcements, ethics are situational at best.

There are signs to look for that suggest your employees are dissatisfied with the integrity of their workplace. These signs point to the fact that a leader is adversely affecting company morale. First, as I said before, loyalty is tied to integrity. If you have a high turnover rate, chances are that something is wrong. Although it is easy to make excuses, it may be that you are to blame. There may be a number of reasons why people are unhappy at their jobs. However, if you are seeing higher numbers of workers leaving, it is definitely time to take a look at the organization's overall integrity, including your own.

Low productivity or morale and increased absenteeism are also signs that something is amiss. When people are unhappy, they do not work as productively. You should investigate the causes of such behavior even if it is not related to ethical concerns. Finally, look for signs that employees are not comfortable approaching you. If they do not seek you out for answers or to talk, something is wrong. Check to make sure that employees are sharing information with you. If you are not receiving any feedback and employees are avoiding you, you have a bad situation brewing.

Chapter Analysis

Keys to Understanding

- For everyone, honesty really is the best policy.

- Just because you are being honest does not mean that you cannot be gentle and empathetic.

- The integrity of the leader and organization is directly related to employee happiness, productivity, and loyalty.

Questions for Reflection

1. What are some aspects of integrity besides honesty?

2. What does your organization do to promote integrity?

3. What behaviors are you using to demonstrate integrity?

4. Do you see any contradictions between your personal ethics and your actions? How about within the organization as a whole?

Chapter 32

Micromanaging Away Imagination, Innovation, and Individuality

Never tell people how to do things. Tell them what to do, and they will surprise you with their ingenuity.

–George Patton

Leaders should recognize that workers know a great deal more about their jobs than anyone else, including the leader. Perhaps the leader may have done that job in the past, but that does not mean it is done the same way now. Also, leaders need to recognize that not everyone does things in the same way.

People have methods that work best for them personally, and they need to be able to have some control over how they accomplish a task. Some people's instincts dictate that they plan out how they will accomplish a task step by step, and then they follow this plan sequentially. Some people do their best work at the last minute, under pressure of a deadline. Sometimes, bosses label these people. They call people who work at the last minute procrastinators or lazy. However, when bosses do this, they have failed to recognize that each person has an individual, natural style of doing things. To reach their full potential, employees must be allowed to work within their own natural styles.

Rather than make your employees adapt to how you do things, you should lead them in regards to how they work.

If one person needs specific instructions and a clear plan on how to accomplish a task, you need to supply that. If another person needs space to create a more individual plan then that should be acceptable, too. You will have much more productive workers if you manage them by their style and not your own.

Smart leaders give clear direction to their people, telling them what they want done and when they need it accomplished. Any other restrictions should be stated up front. Other than that, capable workers should be allowed to use their own creativity to get the job done. Most people do not appreciate your standing over them while they work and critiquing every move or idea. This is a waste of time and an annoyance to your employees. If you do not feel comfortable letting a person do an assigned task without your constant supervision, then perhaps you should not assign that particular task to that person.

On the other hand, you may be letting your ego convince you that nothing can get done without your input. Do not be arrogant enough to believe that no one can have valuable ideas except for you. You really want to avoid the tendency of making people follow your style rather than their own. Keep this in mind when you are managing your employees. Let them work in the style that is right for them. They do not have to do things exactly as you do. Chances are that the way in which you work is incorrect or even disastrous for them.

I once had a job where I had to represent my boss at important meetings when he was unavailable. One time, I told him that although I certainly didn't mind going to the meetings, it was harder for me to go than it was for him. When he asked why, I told him that when he went to the meetings, all he had to do was say whatever he thought about any issue that came up. However, when I attended the meetings, I had to try and say *what I thought he would have said.*

This was the type of boss who wanted things said and done exactly the way he would have done them. This is a difficult task because there are a lot of different ways to get the job done correctly. As a leader, you should try and avoid narrowing the path of your people. They do not always need to take the one that you would have traveled. If you allow creativity, you will get creativity. Otherwise, you create oppression and resentment, and this makes it impossible to reach an organization's highest potential.

Chapter Analysis

Keys to Understanding

- Avoid "micromanagement" and recognize that there may be many different ways to do a job successfully.

- If you remove your ego and feelings of self-importance, you may find that your subordinates have found a clever way of doing the job, perhaps even better than the way you had in mind.

Questions for Reflection

1. Is "micromanagement" a relative term? How is it defined?

2. How do you distinguish between "micromanaging" and being explicit?

3. At what point or under what circumstances is "micromanagement" desirable?

4. When does one put the reins on "how" a job is done?

Chapter 33

Motivating Others

People are born equal but they are also born different.

−Erich Fromm

One of the greatest failures of leaders is attempting to use the same motivators for all employees. The fact is that all people do not want the same things. Therefore, they are not all motivated by the same incentives. Leaders often assume that what personally motivates them now or what has motivated them in the past will be effective motivating factors for everyone.

As a leader you should first be concerned with eliminating factors that can negatively impact motivation. These factors could include things such as poor working conditions, inadequate equipment, or lack of knowledge. Workers will not be motivated to perform well when the essentials that their jobs require are absent. Only when the basics are in place can a leader attempt to make a positive impact on motivation.

Real motivation comes from within. Everyone has a certain natural capacity for motivation. This ebbs and flows over the years, depending on a variety of different factors. For each person, at a different time in life, there will be certain factors that are more dominant and factors that have no effect.

Abraham Maslow, a leader of the humanistic school of psychology, devised a "hierarchy of needs." It puts the basic needs, such as housing and food, at the bottom of the pyramid and self-actualization at the highest level. In between there are a myriad of factors. Consider just a few: position, title, pay, incentive, compensation, working hours, benefits, office, responsibilities, recognition, coworkers, and "perks."

Many of these factors are things over which you do have some control as a leader. You can have an impact on employees' levels of motivation. But in order to be successful, you must analyze your employees and know what each person wants and values. It makes no sense to use a motivator that has no material impact. Once you know what will motivate employees best, you can begin to use positive reinforcement to encourage them. Remember that everyone is motivated by different concerns. They may value money, security, or respect. Others may value flexibility, recognition, or self-expression. Leaders often fail to motivate others because they assume that what works for them is what will motivate their employees. You must identify what factors reinforce your employees to work to their highest potential.

Finding out what will motivate employees is not a simple task, but the first step is simple – you ask them. You may find that even a casual conversation reveals a lot about how employees view various motivational factors. Also, pay attention to how they work and what they like to do. If there is a particular job that someone likes, you can use this as a reward. It can also work in the opposite direction. If there is a task that someone really dislikes, assigning it to someone else can be a positive reinforcement. Once you have given a reward, watch to see how it influences performance. If quality and amount of production increase, it was a good motivator. In this experimental manner, you can judge what motivates and what does not. You can then adjust your actions accordingly.

There are a few more points to discuss regarding motivation. First, hire people that have demonstrated a high level of motivation in their life and in their work history. These people are probably driven by nature if their backgrounds suggest a great deal of achievement. Secondly, do everything within your power to create a work environment that will allow people to motivate themselves. Let them know that there will be rewards for optimal performance. Promotions, recognition, or raises are all long-term goals that keep most people focused on working hard. Finally, once you have done this and certain individuals still cannot be motivated, it may be time to have a sincere talk with these employees about their ability to continue on in the organization.

Employee Motivators

There are many factors that can motivate employees. Everyone is different in regards to what motivates them and why. As a leader, you can have an impact on your employees' attitudes. Begin by evaluating your organization. Look to see if key motivators are present. Here are some of the most important things people want out of their jobs:

✓ Possibility for growth and development

✓ Potential for advancement

✓ Responsibilities

✓ Recognition and respect

✓ Meaningful work that allows for self-expression

✓ Demonstrated concern from their leaders and organization

✓ Positive work environment

✓ An organization that conducts itself morally and with integrity

Chapter Analysis

Keys to Understanding

- As a leader, try to stay informed as to your people's levels of motivation.

- Ensure that you are not an impediment to their ability to stay motivated.

- Reward your motivated employees continuously.

Questions for Reflection

1. How do you know what each person wants and values? How do you go about finding out this information?

2. What are the things that motivate you? Why? How have these things changed over time?

3. What motivating factors are present within your organization? Which are absent?

Chapter 34

Empowerment and Delegation

In an empowered organization there are bound to be a lot more disagreements because we value open and direct communication; we give people permission to disagree.

–Robert Hass, CEO Levi Strauss

Empowerment is one of the big buzzwords used in management circles. It is also one of the most subverted and abused words currently in usage. Are there any managers currently working who will say that they do *not* empower their employees? If there are, I haven't met them. True employee empowerment comes when you delegate responsibilities so that employees can grow in their skills and knowledge.

Delegation is the only way to efficiently manage an organization. Leaders must realize that there is only so much time, and they cannot possibly do everything themselves. Delegation requires balance. You must take into consideration the situation at hand and the abilities and the skill levels of your employees.

When you delegate too much responsibility, employees may feel overloaded and incapable of handling the task. This sets them up for failure. If you do not delegate enough, employees do not have a sense of personal involvement in their jobs. When employees have a sense of control over their responsibilities and organizational decisions, they feel empowered.

The problem with empowerment is not the concept. The problems start during the application stage. The concept puts forward that employees should be trusted and decisions should be pushed down to the lowest appropriate level. It involves risk on the part of the organization and requires management to be supportive during both successes and failures. It gives more power to people in the lower levels of the organization than they ordinarily have in a traditional management hierarchy.

It sounds good, doesn't it? It sure does to me. Unfortunately though, managers have a tendency to butcher this concept into an unrecognizable state. The first problem is a lack of trust regarding employees. Although most managers would not admit it, many do not really trust their employees. They see it as their job to catch people doing something wrong. They also feel that unless employees are being watched, they will not work properly. Although this may be true from time to time, many managers feel it is true in all cases. They do not think that employees would make good decisions if left on their own. If you hire wisely and think through the delegation process before you begin it, this mistrust will lessen. Employees need to have the confidence that their leader believes in their skills and judgment.

The second problem involves risk taking. Giving more power to lower-level employees is potentially dangerous. If they do not use the power properly and wisely, many things can go wrong. Some managers do not want to be involved in such risky situations and are not about to give up control over the outcome of a situation.

The third problem involves failure. When employees are empowered, there are going to be the inevitable cases of failure. There will also be an immense amount of progress. Many managers like to assess blame when something goes wrong, fearing that errors will reflect on their own performance. They do not view failure as a potential steppingstone to success.

They may also see failing to maintain control over the organization as their own failure. They see it as a weakness that they need to rely on others.

Leaders who say they empower their employees need to understand the entire concept. It involves giving employees high levels of trust, understanding the attendant risks, and accepting failure in stride. If a leader is unwilling or unable to fully accept this notion, their "empowerment" is just a facade with no real substance.

In *The Secret of a Winning Culture*, Senn and Childress state, "The kind of empowerment that creates exceptional results is made up of two major elements: the letting go of tight controls by leadership and the acceptance of personal accountability by all employees." These two elements work together to form the essence of successful empowerment.

Leaders must first decide when they are going to involve workers through delegation and to what extent they will do so. To begin, you must decide which employees are capable of taking on the added responsibilities. Delegation works best when you pick the right employee. Not all employees are interested in or have the ability to be involved in the process. Most workers enjoy responsibility and the chance to build their skills, but others simply want to be told what to do and then do it.

The employees you select should understand and agree with the major goals of the organization. They should have experience relating to the situation and, if possible, previous involvement making decisions. They must have an understanding of the situation and an interest in it and its resolution. You should select people who are autonomous and seek out responsibility. People who need firm directions may not thrive under these conditions because these situations inherently involve a level of uncertainty. If you choose the right person, delegation has a high probability of succeeding. In the end, you will have more experienced employees who will be able to handle even more responsibility.

The leader's own style also plays a part in how delegation occurs. Some leaders believe that workers should have a large amount of participation in the workplace, while others see this as shirking responsibility on their parts. Leaders with a high tolerance for uncertainty have an easier time delegating assignments. They must be able to release some control over the outcome of the situation when they delegate it to someone else. Also, some leaders are naturally more comfortable sharing decisions and working with employees. Others are more inclined to solve problems on their own and order others in a more structured way.

The task must also be contemplated when deciding to assign it to a worker. Some jobs are more easily delegated than others. If the problem is commonly known throughout the organization and its outcome will directly affect the work of employees, their input can be valuable and necessary.

You must also understand that shared decision making takes more time than authoritative leadership does. In the long-term view, delegating work will save you time because you will not have to do all the work by yourself. However, if it is a crisis situation where decisions must be made quickly, it may be best to keep the task for yourself.

Empowering workers through delegation is best done a little at a time. As the employee's skills and knowledge increase, you can feel more comfortable giving them more responsibilities. When delegating a task, give clear, precise directions on what is to be accomplished. Also, let employees know when you need it completed and any applicable restrictions. Check to make sure that the employees understand the task at hand.

The first time an employee performs a new responsibility, you can walk through it with the person, seeking his or her ideas on what to do before sharing your own. It is okay to let the person know what you would do but be sure to communicate the fact that you respect other views. Let the person know that you are there should help be needed and that you realize that failure is a possibility. Afterwards, follow through with the assignment and the employee to make certain that everything ran smoothly and was accomplished.

Empowerment of employees has many far-reaching benefits for the organization. When there is a strong delineation between management and employee responsibilities, it stifles the creativity and motivation of workers. They feel that they should only do what they are told to do and nothing more. They do not think outside of their own job description. Empowerment motivates workers and gives them a sense of accomplishment.

When you do not delegate any responsibilities, you can frustrate and anger employees. This may lead to negative attitudes, apathy, and high turnover rates. It creates an oppressive workplace where creativity, imagination, and innovation are stifled. In such an environment, the most talented people will leave for better opportunities. Trying to do everything, the leader will become stressed and lose sight of the organization's direction. Major initiatives may be put aside because the leader is focused on all the minute details. This myopia can lead the organization to failure.

Empowerment and delegation can improve the quality of work and decisions simply because there is more than one perspective involved. Office relations may be improved because a sense of cooperation is incorporated into the group dynamic. Individuals develop because they are allowed the chance to grow and learn. All of these results will have a long-term positive impact on your organization.

Chapter Analysis

Keys to Understanding

- When used properly, empowerment is an outstanding leadership device.

- If you empower your employees, you will have great successes but also the potential for more failures. Recognize this and accept it as a natural part of empowerment.

- You must carefully decide when and to what extent you will delegate responsibility to employees. Many issues must be considered before making this decision.

- Delegation leads to empowerment, which is very beneficial to any organization.

Questions for Reflection

1. Where is the point between delegation and organizational anarchy? Is there a difference between managing and leading?

2. Do you secretly distrust your employees' abilities to make the right decisions? Do you perceive that things will turn out wrong?

3. What are the hidden costs of empowerment? What are the rewards?

4. What are the differences between empowerment and consensus management?

Chapter
35

Attitude

There is little difference in people, but that little difference makes a big difference. The little difference is attitude. The big difference is whether it is positive or negative.

−Clement Stone

I have never seen a monument erected to a pessimist.

−Paul Harvey

There are days when I come to work, and I am not feeling my best. My goal on those days is to act in such a way that no one is able to identify that I am not in top form. I do this because I take my position very seriously. I feel that I have a responsibility to be upbeat, even when I'm not. Most leaders do not appreciate how much they impact people. If the boss is clearly having a bad day, it can become a bad day for the entire organization. As a leader, you are part cheerleader, and you never see an "on-duty" cheerleader in a bad mood.

This is not an easy burden to bear. Kouzes and Posner have researched this issue, and in *The Leadership Challenge*, they state that many leaders describe "putting on a happy face each morning" as one of the most difficult, exhausting, and crucial performance requirements of the job. Despite the burden, good leaders do this every day. There is a payoff: fewer bad moods within management mean fewer throughout the organization.

Maintaining a good mood, even when you do not feel it, does not have to mean lying to employees or being deceitful.

You can be honest and forthright when there are factors that may impair your ability to be a good leader. However, staying upbeat means that you do not complain about the little things, and you certainly do not complain to your workers.

If you are feeling stressed, find some ways to relax and rejuvenate. If you need to voice concerns over policies, decisions, etc., do so to your supervisor or someone who holds the same or higher level of authority as you do. Complaints of this nature should run up the chain of command not down. When you walk around, keep a smile on your face. Don't let body language give away how you feel inside. These tactics allow you to maintain a positive, up-beat, team-oriented image in the eyes of your workers. Surprisingly, research shows that if you act upbeat, chances are that you will begin feeling that way.

Chapter
Analysis

Keys to Understanding

- Be cognizant of your moods and the impact they can have on your organization.

- Always strive to put forward a positive attitude and an upbeat demeanor. If you cannot do this, how can you expect it from your employees?

Questions for Reflection

1. To what extent does your mood affect the organization?

2. How can a leader "fake it" by exhibiting a good attitude even when that is not the case and still remain "genuine" with the staff and retain integrity?

3. What is the difference between a good attitude and the "cheerleader" attitude?

Chapter 36

Fairness

*Men are by nature unequal. It is vain, therefore,
to treat them as if they were equal.*

–J.A. Froude

Favoritism is one of the most frequent complaints
workers have about management. All leaders are human
beings. It is natural to have likes and dislikes, and this
extends to people as well. As a leader, you must distance
yourself as much as possible from becoming too intimate
with employees or letting your feelings dictate how you
behave. Decisions should not be based on how you feel
about a person. You are paid to be objective and take into
account all sides of an issue.

I have had to handle numerous disciplinary cases in
my career. Normally, it is my responsibility to review the
misconduct in question and recommend a consequence to
the chief executive. There have been several instances when I
have supported employees on one issue when, on the whole, I
felt they were undeserving based upon past conduct. I was
able to separate my personal feelings about the person from
the individual facts of the current case.

I have even had other managers question my decision
because they knew the employee had behaved inappropriately
in the past. I feel strongly, however, that this is the way to be
fair consistently. The same is true in reverse when you have
to take harsh action against someone you really respect.

In their book, *Putting Total Quality Management to Work*, Marshall Sashkin and Kenneth Kiser list ten specific areas of action that help to create an organizational climate of fairness:

1. Actions that develop trust, such as sharing useful information and making good on commitments

2. Acting consistently, so that employees are not surprised or taken aback by unexpected management actions or decisions

3. Being scrupulously truthful and avoiding "white lies"

4. Demonstrating integrity by keeping confidences and observing ethical guidelines to show concern for others

5. Meeting with employees and defining what is expected of them

6. Treating employees equitably and not playing favorites

7. Giving people meaningful influence over decisions about their own work, especially how to accomplish their work

8. Adhering to clear standards that are just and reasonable

9. Demonstrating respect toward employees

10. Following due process, or procedures that are open to public scrutiny and that permit everyone to participate actively in their application

◊

A great deal may be done by severity, more by love, but most by clear discernment and impartial justice.

–Goethe

◊

Chapter Analysis

Keys to Understanding

- Try to incorporate fairness into every action you take.

- Any bias, positive or negative, you may have regarding an individual should not determine your decisions.

- People really look for and respond to fair leaders.

Questions for Reflection

1. How can a leader be detached and fair but not present the appearance of being distant and unapproachable?

2. Does your organization foster fairness and just and reasonable standards that are made public?

3. Review Sashkin and Kiser's list: are any of the components missing from your organization?

Chapter 37

Praise and Criticism

Sandwich every bit of criticism between two layers of praise.

–Mary Kay Ash

I have yet to find a man, whatever his situation in life, who did not do better work and put forth greater effort under a spirit of approval than he ever would do under a spirit of criticism.

–Charles Schwab

Ken Blanchard and Spencer Johnson make some interesting observations about criticism and praise in their book, *The One Minute Manager.* They recommend that praise be given when someone does something *approximately* right. Their contention is that if we wait for perfection in order to praise, we will never praise.

There are some key factors to remember that will make criticism easier to give and easier to take. First, when you criticize, start with the positive, such as examples of what has been done well. Then pinpoint what needs to be done differently. Try to end on a positive note. Secondly, reprimands should be brief and timely. Negative behavior needs to be corrected as quickly as possible. You should not gather up negative information over time and then bring it to someone's attention all at once. There is less chance that the behavior will actually be corrected if a person cannot remember it. Reprimanding a whole list of wrong doings at once will send the message to that person that nothing they do is right. Try to stick to one point at a time.

Blanchard and Johnson remind us that we are reprimanding behavior and not the person. People should walk
away from a conversation thinking about their own behavior,
not the behavior of the boss. By reprimanding the behavior
and not the person, you create a better chance that the person
will actually consider what was done incorrectly and how to
improve. When you are aggressive or offensive while cor-
recting behavior, you put people on the defensive. They are
focusing on their feelings and not what needs to be done. You
have defeated the true purpose of the correction.

I have never been hesitant to criticize someone, and I
have always been willing to praise. People who have been
praised in the past will be more open to criticism because they
trust that your intentions are good. When you do have to
criticize them, there will be an overall balance of praise and
criticism. They will be more open to the suggestion because
you have dealt out both praise and reprimand equally and
honestly.

Remember the old rule about criticizing someone's
performance: praise in public and reprimand in private.
The object of criticism is not to embarrass but to improve
performance. There have been occasions, though, where I
reprimanded someone in front of others. This is only for
extreme cases where someone is just refusing to follow directions properly. I do not like to use this method, but when all
else fails, I have found it to be incredibly effective. Under normal
circumstances, this is unnecessary and unprofessional.
Corrections should be between you and the other people
involved; the entire staff does not need to be included. Use
this technique only as a last resort.

When you criticize, you should be constructive and
precise. To tell people that they have bad attitudes may be a
true statement, but you must elaborate. Explain to them
exactly which of their behaviors leads you to the belief that
they have attitude problems. This is not always easy because

sometimes the problem, like a bad attitude, is hard to identify and hard to describe. Specific criticism helps employees to understand precisely what you expect and what they need to do to meet your expectations. It is also helpful to explain why the correction is needed. If people do not understand why something needs to be done differently, they are less likely to change. Also, let employees participate in discussions on how to make corrections. Get people to think of their own ways to improve so that they are more personally involved in the matter.

Finally, be as gentle as possible with your criticism. Consider how you would want to be given criticism. Words can injure deeply, and although you may not see the damage visibly, it can be quite devastating. Leaders have more impact with their words than they realize. People are often able to recount in great detail criticism they received from their bosses a decade ago. Do not be afraid to criticize but think about it beforehand and choose your words very carefully.

You want to create a workplace where criticism is given constructively. You should never allow mean-spirited or vindictive motives to pervade criticism. This is true when you or your employees critique others. When everyone in the workplace feels that criticism is being given honestly and by people who care for one another, the potential for improvement is unlimited. Share these steps on how to criticize constructively with your employees. If everyone understands how to criticize in a productive manner, your workplace will be a healthy environment where improvements can take place.

A final word on criticism comes from this story about Jay Leno's effort to keep criticism in the proper perspective:

When Jay Leno replaced Johnny Carson on *The Tonight Show*, he started to take some heat. Critics unfavorably compared him to Johnny, and from all that criticism, most people thought his stay as the host would be short-lived. However, Jay never really worried. In fact, he kept a stack of unpleasant reviews on his desk for inspiration. One critic said, "Too many soft questions." Another said, "He's being too nice." These unkind words did not bother Leno though because they were written in 1962 and were directed at Jack Paar's replacement – "an awkward nobody named Johnny Carson."

Remember that being the boss is not just about reprimanding mistakes. Too often, we focus solely on the negative. Blanchard and Johnson recommend that you try to acknowledge someone doing something *right*. When this occurs, let the employee know that you noticed it and reward the person accordingly. Most people do not mind working hard. However, they become frustrated when no one seems to appreciate their efforts. Lack of appreciation is a dangerous thing that can quickly destroy employee morale. All people hope for certain rewards in return for their work. If they don't receive them, they become discouraged.

Some managers operate with the attitude that people are getting paid, and that is all the reward they need. The effect of this is potentially demoralizing. People that feel their efforts are not being recognized may begin to develop resentment toward their job, which in turn can impact the quantity and quality of their work. Unhappy and neglected workers are not productive.

◊

When a man points a finger at someone else, he should remember that three of his fingers are pointing at himself.
–Anonymous
◊

Chapter Analysis

Keys to Understanding

- Balance criticism with praise.

- Criticize behavior and not the person.

- Be specific in your criticisms.

- When criticizing, be as gentle as possible. The power of your words as a leader cannot be overestimated.

Questions for Reflection

1. How do you criticize the behavior but not the person?

2. Does an environment of honest criticism lead to productive improvements?

3. What is the balance or ratio between criticism and praise in your organization?

Chapter
38

Empathy

One of the most poignant of all human experiences is empathy — the ability to feel what others feel when suffering from pain or loss.

–Louis West

Not everyone has a good capacity for empathy, as shown in this story:

Many years ago, a preacher from Kansas was returning home after a visit to New England, and one of his parishioners met him at the train station. "Well," asked the preacher, "how are things at home?" "Sad, real sad Pastor," answered the man. "A tornado came and wiped out my house." "Well, I'm not surprised," said the unsympathetic preacher. "You remember I've been warning you about the way you've been living. Punishment for sin is inevitable." The layman responded, "It also destroyed your house, Pastor." "It did?" the pastor asked, momentarily surprised. "Oh my, the ways of the Lord are past human understanding."

Many people lose empathy when they become leaders. Some never had the capacity for it in the first place. Being in a powerful leadership position can make people susceptible to memory loss. They seemingly cannot recall how it felt to be in certain situations. It is difficult to relate to your employees if you do not remember being one.

The best leaders are the ones who have not lost their ability to be empathetic. Empathy is not something you pull out when needed. It is something that pervades everything you do as a leader. It impacts how you treat people, how you talk to people, and the level of care you have for people. In short, it impacts every human interaction you have and any managerial action you must take.

Having empathy for workers does not preclude you from making hard decisions or taking tough action. It is merely one component of an overall approach. In some cases, you may take the exact same measures, regardless of whether or not you are concerned for the individuals involved. However, if you have strong empathy for people, you will find that it will occasionally sway your decisions. Being empathetic will also change the way that you implement decisions. That may be just as important as the decision itself.

How does a leader develop empathy? The easiest way is to consciously analyze how a particular decision would make you feel if you were in the same situation. That's the classical Golden Rule approach, and while somewhat useful, it has many drawbacks. To truly be empathetic, you must be aware of a person's complete background, history, education, culture, morals, social position, financial status, interests, thinking patterns, and social status. It is virtually impossible to really do that; we can only hope to approximate it.

Being aware of the culturally diverse nature of the workplace is a first step. Becoming informed of the differences and nuances of different cultures is another step. Finally, being sensitive to the position and social dynamics at play makes a leader more effective at employing empathy as a powerful ingredient in decisions.

Chapter Analysis

Keys to Understanding

- Strive to retain your empathy.

- Empathy pervades almost every human interaction a leader has. Recognize its importance in your role.

Questions for Reflection

1. How prominent do you feel empathy is in your management style?

2. Where does one draw the line at empathy?

3. Can an empathetic leader appear weak?

4. How do you demonstrate empathy toward your employees? What do you think their perception is of you as an empathetic leader?

Fun on the Job

The supreme accomplishment is to blur the line between work and play.

–Arnold Toynbee

Work like you don't need the money, love like you've never been hurt, and dance like you do when nobody's watching.

–Anonymous

I have had the great pleasure of meeting and talking with four of the twelve men who have walked on the moon. As a space enthusiast, I had many questions for each of them. There was a common theme among their answers that struck me. The theme was best summed up by what the late Pete Conrad told me as I spoke of his heroics. He said, "We weren't so great; we just did what we had fun doing."

In my view, the space program and the moon landings were the greatest and most audacious human efforts ever. The training requirements and pressures put on these men were enormous. They were literally putting their lives at risk, but they viewed it as merely having fun. If under such serious conditions these men can perceive their work as fun, I think it is okay for the rest of us to do so.

I have worked for bosses who thought that it was their job to ensure that people were not having fun. They perceived that more fun would equal less work. I have also worked for a boss who practically demanded that we enjoyed ourselves. In his estimation, work should be pleasurable.

He thought that if you were having fun at what you did, you would be happier and work more productively.

I agree that work can and should be fun. Granted, there are some jobs that lend themselves to this more than others. However, I think every boss would do well to make the work environment fun and exciting. This means that amusement and laughter should not be foreign to the workplace. Happy people truly are more vital, creative, and productive. They have more personal concern for the organization, and therefore, they work harder to accomplish its goals.

The more people enjoy their work and environment, the more likely it is that they will stay with the organization. Happy and fulfilled employees tend to be more loyal and dedicated. Absenteeism and employee turnover are also reduced. So, all you leaders, keep repeating after me, "It's okay to have fun at work, it's okay to have fun at work…"

The perceptive leader can distinguish between a healthy amount of fun and the point at which having fun tends to disrupt the production. The line is almost imperceptible, but once crossed, it can negatively influence morale. That probably accounts for some leaders' fear of allowing any joviality; they don't know where the line is and are fearful of finding out that they have crossed it inadvertently. The art of leadership involves feeling confident enough in your judgment to know the limit and having enough faith in your employees to know they won't abuse it.

Chapter Analysis

Keys to Understanding

- People who are having fun at work will probably work harder and produce better-quality material.
- You should encourage fun, laughter, and camaraderie to the greatest extent possible.

Questions for Reflection

1. How much laughter occurs at your workplace? Is it conducive to a productive environment? Does it encourage employee loyalty?
2. Where is the "fun-at-work" line drawn? Why?
3. What is the distinction between having fun working and having fun at work?

Chapter 40

Developing People

Treat people as if they were what they ought to be and you help them become what they are capable of becoming.

−Goethe

To teach is to learn twice.

−Joseph Joubert

In *Managing People is like Herding Cats*, Bennis stated that the organizations that would succeed were those who believed that their competitive advantage depended on their people. These organizations would constantly develop their employees and take actions designed to improve the quality and morale of the employees.

People are the most important resource in any organization. From a purely financial standpoint, employee salaries are a huge part of any company's budget. This valuable resource must be managed wisely and effectively. I believe in constantly teaching, training, and mentoring workers. It is key to enhancing productivity and increasing morale.

Obviously, employees must be fully trained to do their current jobs. However, they should also be cross-trained for other jobs, thereby increasing their value and versatility. This also helps people to grow into other roles in the organization, including promotional opportunities. Training should be ongoing – you never really "finish" after a cursory initial training period. Continual, verifiable training can also be invaluable to an organization in these litigious times. Many an organization has paid out a huge sum of money in lawsuits filed under the "negligent training" legal theory.

Teaching and training are not just limited to formal courses or seminars. In fact, most of the time, the training and teaching are informal, on the job, and done on a day-by-day basis. If a leader makes training and teaching a priority, this filters down through the organization. Managers and supervisors become mentors and teachers to their employees, and the whole company becomes a "learning organization."

In his book, *Principle-Centered Leadership*, Stephen Covey makes some excellent observations in regard to teaching and training employees:

> Recognize and take time to teach. With differences come supreme teaching moments. But there's a time to teach and a time not to teach. It's time to teach when 1) people are not threatened (efforts to teach when people feel threatened will only increase resentment, so wait for or create a new situation in which the person feels more secure and receptive); 2) you're not angry or frustrated, when you have feelings of affection, respect, and inward security; and 3) when the other person needs help and support (to rush in with success formulas when someone is emotionally low or fatigued or under a lot of pressure is comparable to trying to teach a drowning man to swim). Remember: we are teaching one thing or another all of the time because we are constantly radiating what we are.

Make a commitment to teaching and training your people. It is the best investment any company can make.

◊
Tell me, I'll forget. Show me, I may remember.
But involve me, and I'll understand.
—Chinese Proverb
◊

Chapter Analysis

Keys to Understanding

- Recognize the immense value of your people.

- Develop, teach, and train them at every opportunity.

- Be certain to pick out the best opportunity to teach employees – when they are ready to learn.

- Remember that training is an ongoing, day-to-day process.

Questions for Reflection

1. What is the right amount and type of training that your organization should have? Is it meeting its goals and purposes?

2. How do "lifelong learning" and training differ? Who should take the initiative in training?

Chapter
41

Moral Courage

It is curious, curious that physical courage should be so common in the world, and moral courage so rare.

–Mark Twain

Moral courage is the most valuable and usually the most absent characteristic in men.

–General George Patton

I work in an industry where physical courage is literally part of the job description. I have seen many acts of physical courage over the years. However, I must agree with Mr. Twain; moral courage seems to be more rare.

To be a good leader, you need to have moral courage. What does this mean? Many of the chapters in this book speak of areas in which moral courage must be present in order to be effective. Leaders who are good at making tough decisions and who are honest and fair possess an internal component of moral courage. Moral courage is yet another one of those leadership concepts that is hard to define, but we know it when we see it.

Moral courage is recognizing your values and beliefs and not letting them be compromised regardless of the circumstances. When temptation cannot lead you to abandon your principles, you display such courage. Good leaders do not practice situational ethics but are resolute in their beliefs. You must face the consequences whenever your morals are challenged; either you will protect your values or you will desert them and lose your integrity.

In the capitalistic nature of business, it is easy for some people to lose sight of ethical conduct. They focus so intently on the bottom-line, profits, or expansion that they lose perspective of what is acceptable behavior. Is it acceptable to use sweatshop labor to increase your profit margins; is it okay to pollute the environment in order to reduce costs?

These are large, complex issues that leaders face, but you must also remember to recognize the smaller, daily questions of moral behavior. Will you speak up when someone is being treated unfairly? Will you look the other way when others use expense accounts for their own personal use? Moral courage involves not only knowing what you stand for but also actually standing up for it.

Perhaps the greatest lack of moral courage I have ever observed came many years ago in a personnel matter. A loyal, long-time employee was to be fired. Although there were some performance problems involved, politics involving the leader's personal favorites were really the driving force behind the termination.

It was the responsibility of the leader to notify the employee. This particular manager's level of moral courage was not his strongest point. Instead of facing the employee, the manager called in an outside organizational consultant to do it! He couldn't stand up and do the job because of his own lack of moral integrity. His shameful lack of moral courage was extreme; unfortunately, similar things happen in organizations frequently.

If you are in a leadership position, understand that having the moral courage to take the right action is another requirement of the job. If you are not comfortable doing so, please do not voluntarily allow yourself to be placed in a position of leading people. You will only be tormented, and your people will suffer.

The ultimate example of courage was demonstrated by the courageous passengers aboard United Airlines Flight 93 on September 11, 2001. These individuals showed bravery above and beyond what any of us will probably ever have to face. When they discovered that their plane was hijacked with the possible intention of crashing it into a populated area, a small group banded together to try to potentially save thousands of lives. Knowing that it would be their last act, they attempted to overtake the plane before it could be used to cause the death of even more people.

These passengers displayed the highest form of heroism – to die for the noblest of causes. The number of lives they saved that day cannot be measured and neither can the amount of bravery that they demonstrated. They will forever be remembered as examples of true heroes who faced adversity, fear, and death with dignity and courage and chose to rise above their circumstances.

Chapter Analysis

Keys to Understanding

- In order to have credibility as a leader, you must possess and display moral courage.
- Some leadership positions require physical courage but all require moral courage.

Questions for Reflection

1. How do you define moral courage? Think of situations that require it.
2. Can moral courage be learned?

Supporting People

The best leaders are those most interested in surrounding themselves with assistants and associates smarter than they are — being frank in admitting this — and willing to pay for such talents.

–Amos Parrish

A long time ago, when I was relatively new to the workplace, a supervisor told me that as long as I was right, he would support me. Even as a newcomer, I recognized that if I was right about something, I would not necessarily need his support. The times that I would need his support would be the times when I was wrong. This meant that the only time I would receive the support of this supervisor was when I did not really need that support.

I am afraid that not much has changed in the way some leaders choose to give or withhold their support. It is important to support your employees at all times, especially when they are wrong. That does not mean you must always support the behavior. Remember that when workers make mistakes, you can disapprove of the behavior but still support the people. Let them know that what they did was incorrect but that you still believe in their ability to do a good job.

Likewise, if you cannot support a person, let your reasons be known so that the person can avoid the same mistakes in the future. You should, however, support the worker if that person was making an honest attempt to do the job properly. When you do not support your employees and put obstacles in their path instead of removing them, you are asking for a frustrated, angry workforce.

This type of frustration is exhibited in this incident:

> Upon receiving a claim from a woman, an insurance company asked her for some additional evidence concerning her husband's death. After a good deal of correspondence, the firm received the following letter from the widow: "I am having such a lot of trouble getting my money that sometimes I actually wish my husband were not dead."

A leader has the responsibility to support people so that they do not end up feeling upset and frustrated. It doesn't take much to make their jobs easier and less stressful in many ways. Speaking up for them or standing beside them during problematic times are the "big ways" leaders lend their support. There are many minor, day-to-day actions that you can take to make a better workplace. Bringing donuts occasionally or sometimes letting an employee off early does wonders for morale. Supporting birthday and anniversary celebrations is another positive action. Even something as small as buying fresh flowers for the office every so often can demonstrate your support.

One of the most important ways you support your staff is by listening to them. Listen to what your workers have to say about their needs because they have a better understanding of them than you will. When they need something to do their jobs, work as hard as you can to produce this for them. This includes such things as equipment, training, or information. It may also include funding or approval from the organization to take on a project. Helping with the little things that make their day run more smoothly demonstrates your support.

A leader will also be called upon to give emotional or technical support. Being a good listener or helping to solve a difficult problem lets your employees know that you care and stand behind them. Support can come in many forms, but it always helps employees be more productive.

Chapter Analysis

Keys to Understanding

- Support your people when they are wrong as well as when they are right. If the person had honorable intentions, condemn the behavior but not the person.

- If you cannot support someone in a given case, be honest with that person. Let your reasons be known.

- Support comes in many different forms.

Questions for Reflection

1. How do you support a person when they have made a mistake or error and need correction? How do you support a person and discipline them for unacceptable behavior?

2. How do you support a person with active listening?

Chapter 42 Worksheet:
How Well Do You Treat Others?

Yes No

☐ ☐ 1. I am thoughtful and sensitive when it comes to others.

☐ ☐ 2. I respect the individuality and opinions of my employees.

☐ ☐ 3. I listen actively to what they say; I devote my full attention to what we are discussing.

☐ ☐ 4. I am attentive and responsive to their needs and desires.

☐ ☐ 5. I am flexible and willing to work together to find solutions.

☐ ☐ 6. I help them to resolve problems.

☐ ☐ 7. I share with my employees, both personally and professionally.

☐ ☐ 8. I am a coach and a cheerleader; I motivate and counsel.

☐ ☐ 9. I communicate goals, problems, and objectives clearly. I discuss these situations with employees.

☐ ☐ 10. I give both positive criticism and praise regularly.

☐ ☐ 11. I am easily accessible to my workers; I spend a large amount of my time interacting with them.

☐ ☐ 12. I am reliable, and I keep my commitments to others.

** As you answer these questions, you should think about what the people in your life would have answered about you. Do you display these behaviors, and if so, how often? You should have answered yes to at least eight of these questions. Otherwise, examine where you could improve.

Chapter 43

Active Management

Good management consists of showing average people how to do the work of superior people.

–John Rockefeller

Leaders must take an active approach toward management. It is your job to know what is going on in the organization. There are many ways to stay informed and communicate with employees. I use an approach called "managing by wandering around" (MBWA), a superb management technique put forward by Tom Peters. The essence of this technique is that managers get out of their offices and find out what is happening in the workplace. Managers will obtain more accurate and timely information and use this to make positive improvements. The key is for managers to follow up on the information they receive.

The MBWA concept is great, but only if it is applied properly. Many managers were under the impression that if they went out, roamed around, and made small talk, they had effectively done their MBWA for the day. They missed the point. There are several critical components to MBWA. First, it must be done with sincerity. If you are not speaking with employees from a sincere standpoint, it will show, and it will backfire on you. If you really do not want to use MBWA, then don't. Insincerity is a waste of time and rarely fools anyone.

Secondly, you must be working to elicit more than surface feedback. Initially, employees will probably provide very superficial information. You have to take the time to get the "good stuff." MBWA is not something to be done once a month on Tuesdays between 3:00 and 4:00 p.m. It is a perpetual, ongoing process. Once it has begun, it never ends.

You must also be responsive to what you are told. If someone tells you that they need a particular piece of equipment, get it for them. If they need some additional training, get it for them. If you sense that they need some recognition, give it to them. Feedback is not worth gathering if you do not do something with that information once you have obtained it. Again, if you are insincere about this process, people recognize it and resent you for it. It is frustrating for you to ask them what they need or what they think but then never do anything about it. Make sure that you are putting effort into responding to their input.

There will be times when you cannot do whatever it is your people ask of you, and that is acceptable. The key is to get back to the employee in a timely fashion. Tell them that you cannot do what it is they would like and give them the reason why if possible. People understand that they will not always get what they want, especially if you give a good reason.

Keys to Active Management

MBWA can be an effective tool when used properly. How you go about gathering information is important. Here are some things to consider as you use an MBWA approach:

✓ MBWA must be ongoing and routine or it is ineffective.

✓ You must approach it with a sincere attitude.

✓ Know on which projects employees are currently working.

✓ Use probing questions. Yes-and-no answers are not going to help you assess problems in the workplace.

✓ Respond to employee feedback. They will be more forthcoming if they know their views shape your actions.

Chapter Analysis

Keys to Understanding

- Either do MBWA properly or don't do it at all.

- If you do MBWA, be sincere and always get back to people with the answers that you promised to give them.

- MBWA is perpetual; it must be done continually to be effective.

Questions for Reflection

1. What are the proper postures, gaits, facial expressions, and attitudes for effective MBWA?

2. How do you pevent supervisors and those reporting to you from feeling resentful or overly scrutinized when you do MBWA?

3. What are the most valuable kinds of information you are likely to get from MBWA?

Morale

*My theory is that an army commander does what is necessary
to accomplish his mission and that 80% of his mission
is to arouse morale in his men.*

–George Patton

Morale is faith in the man at the top.

–Albert Johnstone

Morale is incredibly important in any organization; it
affects everything. It affects how people treat one another,
their work quality, and even the way in which they answer
the phone. It is elusive in nature but palpable in its impact.
If morale is low, it is a problem, even if everything else in an
organization is strong.

High morale creates a more productive workplace.
Employees are enthusiastic, dedicated, and creative. They
have a personal investment in their work and gain a sense of
fulfillment from it. The quality of work and the quality of the
workplace are both increased when morale is high.

In most organizations, management as a whole is collectively responsible for morale. This is fine in theory, but it
does not have a practical application because morale is such an
inclusive and intangible attribute. Through experience, I have
developed a technique that I believe improves morale as a
whole by breaking it down into more manageable pieces. To
explain it, let me illustrate how the technique works for me.

There are three top-level managers who report directly to me. I consider myself responsible for their morale, although I know that I do not have absolute control over it. I ask them regularly about their own morale, and I routinely observe whether they appear to have good morale. I tell them that I will do anything within my power to help their enthusiasm be as high as it can. I have instructed them to inform me if their morale declines between the times when we discuss it it. Therefore, if it is low and they have not informed me, they are literally not following orders!

In turn, these managers are responsible for the people directly below them, the supervisors. I expect that these managers do just as I do with them; they ask their direct subordinates how their morale is and regularly observe it as best they can. If it is low, they are to do anything possible to bring it back up. The supervisors do the same with everyone reporting to them. Supervisors regularly poll employees to gauge their level of morale. The same rules apply. Supervisors have the authority to do what it takes to keep morale high.

I regularly check throughout the entire organization to ensure that my directions have been followed and to make sure that the process is operating as it should. Of course, as one of my supervisors once pointed out, if you are spot-checking, you just might find some spots. I do but not very often.

I am not naive to the point that I think everyone's morale is going to be great. Some people are not happy with their lives in general. How could we possibly expect them to be happy at work? There are probably 10% of the people who are going to be unhappy no matter what. Likewise, there are 10% who are going to be happy no matter what because it is just in their nature. The remaining 80% could go either way depending on the circumstances. Leaders must focus on this group when trying to impact morale.

Although my technique is not the ultimate answer to improving morale, it does lay a good foundation. It requires certain people to be specifically responsible for certain individuals' morale. It also creates regular opportunities for the subject of morale to be discussed. It transforms morale from an intangible, lofty idea to something that can be worked with and examined. Finally, it encourages people to speak out when their morale begins to slip. Sometimes, when you can catch morale problems early, small problems can be prevented from becoming larger ones.

There are some signs to look for that may suggest there are potentially serious, underlying problems with employees and their morale. Employees with low morale levels tend to be late or absent from work more often and may leave early without permission. They may display poor attitudes, act or speak in insubordinate manners, and become argumentative. They may complain more often, make more careless mistakes, and have below- average performance. You should also pay attention to any increase in violations of policy, loss of inventory, missing documents, and cash shortages. There may be abnormal amounts of customer complaints, personal calls and e-mail, and missed deadlines.

What you should watch for is a marked increase in these events and a widespread occurrence of them. One or two people behaving this way may not mean that there are general problems with the organization's overall morale. It may just mean that there is a problem with a limited number of individuals. However, if you notice problems occurring with a large group of people, it is vital to take a closer look. Employee morale is a key component to an organization's productivity; so don't ignore any signs of trouble.

Chapter Analysis

Keys to Understanding

- Morale is one of the most important components in an organization's success.

- A worker's direct supervisor can have the greatest impact on a person's morale.

- Do your best to positively affect morale.

- Ensure that the effort to improve morale pervades the whole organization.

Questions for Reflection

1. What are the major problems that cause a decline in morale?

2. How can a morale check, as outlined in the chapter, go awry? Why?

3. What things do you do as a leader to encourage good morale?

Chapter
45

Building Loyalty

There is one element that is worth its weight in gold and that is loyalty.
It will cover a multitude of weaknesses.

–Phillip Armour

It makes sense that all organizations want their people to be loyal. Managers often fail in this area by expecting that employees will automatically give loyalty. This may be true at the onset of one's career, but as some employees gain more tenure, their loyalty has to be continually earned.

Organizations that do not inspire loyalty in their employees experience a "revolving door" turnover rate. This costs the company time and money because it is continually hiring and training new people. Also, the quality of work and production rates decline when people do not view their job positively. You need loyal people to avoid these problems.

To gain loyalty, leaders must make the first move in good faith. You cannot expect people to be loyal to the organization, if the organization is not first loyal to them. This may not necessarily seem fair, but it is just the way it works.

Creating loyalty is a difficult process. It used to be that loyalty from employees was expected. Unfortunately, that has changed entirely, and today's employee is more likely to be skeptical than loyal. This skepticism is well earned, considering the recent history of organizations being insensitive and callous in their treatment of employees.

People are more willing to stick around if they feel valued and respected in their workplace. Employees must believe in and support the integrity of their organization and work or they are not apt to stay long. They must know that they are your most valued assets. To convey this idea, it is not enough to merely tell them. You must convince them of this fact through your actions and attitudes.

If you want loyalty, the first step is to be loyal. This means being honest with employees, treating them fairly, and taking good care of them, especially during difficult times. If this is what occurs in your organization, then you have every right to expect that people will be loyal. Loyalty is built on a daily basis. Do not think that you can give a raise once a year and keep people loyal. Money or promotions are not the only things that keep people with an organization, and as I discussed before, these may be becoming less significant factors. People want respect, support, and a chance to grow every day that they come into work.

Remember that this is an ongoing effort. There is no law that requires employees to be loyal. It is not really something that can be required. Rather, it is something that must be earned, and it is earned over a period of time as management's actions are compared to rhetoric. All the concepts in this book deal with creating a workplace in which workers are encouraged to trust their employees and thus become loyal. Being a good leader inspires loyalty in your employees. If, through your own example, you have created an ethical organization where employees feel empowered, motivated, respected, and cared for, you are probably well on your way to having employee loyalty.

Chapter Analysis

Keys to Understanding

- Work hard as a leader to earn and maintain your employees' loyalty.

- It is not as difficult to earn loyalty as you might imagine. Once earned, though, there must be an ongoing maintenance effort to retain it.

- Employee loyalty can have drastic effects, either positive or negative, on an organization.

Questions for Reflection

1. What is the difference between morale and loyalty? How are they related, and how are they different?

2. How does trust influence loyalty and morale?

3. Can you, as a leader, do specific things to increase loyalty?

Chapter 46

Anger

It is easy to fly into a passion – anybody can do that – but to be angry with the right person to the right extent and at the right time and with the right object and in the right way – that is not easy, and it is not everyone who can do it.

–Aristotle

When angry, count ten before you speak, if very angry, one hundred.

–Thomas Jefferson

Leaders can get angry the same as anyone else. However, with the privilege of leadership comes responsibility. One of those responsibilities is to maintain control over your temper.

When you are angry you cannot think clearly. The words you choose will tend to be much more abrasive than when you are calm. Harsh words can have long-term, destructive ramifications, particularly with people who are sensitive by nature. Twenty minutes after you were angry, you may have forgotten what you said. I would be willing to bet that people will take longer to forget. They may never forget at all.

This is not to say that you cannot let your employees know when you are angry. No one expects you to be an emotionless robot. Just be cautious when you feel anger starting to rise and do your best to keep it under control. If you are going to express your anger, do it without raising your voice, pounding your fists, or throwing things. If you just have to spout off, remember: a word off the cuff can end up cutting someone terribly. Finding ways to manage your own stress may keep you calmer in the workplace. You have a greater chance of erupting more often if you let things built up without dealing with them.

There are some people who are prone to expressing anger in the workplace and others for whom it is only an occasional occurrence. How do successful leaders avoid problems with anger? Here are some tips:

1. Avoid the "fight" complex. Your body reacts to things going wrong as a threat. You have to intercede and break the pattern so that frustration and anger do not push the violence button. Verbal abuse, tantrums, storming off, and heavy-handed behavior are forms of violence. They have no place in the work environment.

2. When you begin to get angry, remember to take control. Step back and look at the situation from this perspective: what difference will it make in five years?

3. If you begin to get agitated, remember that your adrenaline is flowing. Now is the time for a good brisk walk. Run up five flights of stairs. Work up a sweat. Your body needs to convert the adrenaline or you will have a chemical imbalance that could affect your judgment.

4. As you take your walk, slow down near the end. Pause. Look at the scenery outside. Relax. Remember, whatever the situation, "this too will pass."

5. Meditate and reflect as soon as you are under control and calm. Ask for strength and guidance. Have the assurance that you will make wise choices.

Use these methods and after a while, you will be able to avoid the "fight" complex entirely. Your heartbeat will remain calm under a trying situation. You will come to realize that the situation does not matter, but your reaction to it does. If you can detach yourself far enough to have a long-term perspective, you will be on the way to mastering your emotions. Your confidence will grow because you have achieved self-mastery.

If you feel that your behavior or thoughts are completely out of your control, you may decide to seek the help of a professional. You could speak to a private therapist or, if your organization provides one, to an employee counselor. If you decide that this is the best route available to you, do not feel that this is a weakness on your part or something of which you should be ashamed. True strength is recognizing and admitting that you have a problem and then taking the necessary steps to correct it.

Chapter Analysis

Keys to Understanding

- Keeping your cool pays dividends.

- By remaining calm, people will recognize this as the proper approach and will model that behavior. No one will want to be seen as a hothead if the boss is known for a calm approach.

Questions for Reflection

1. What are some effective ways of dealing with anger in the workplace?

2. How do you deal with a hotheaded subordinate?

3. How do you deal with a boss who is a hothead, and how do you protect your staff from the effects?

4. When is it acceptable to express your anger verbally and have an outburst?

Chapter 47

Stress

*People who cannot find time for recreation are obliged
sooner or later to find time for illness.*

–John Wanamaker

As a leader, you will have to deal with a great amount of stress. Some of it will be externally imposed, and some will be from demands that you impose on yourself. You must first take care of yourself physically and mentally. You cannot effectively lead from the sickbed, and you can only psychologically handle so many things at once.

A certain amount of stress is necessary. You cannot eliminate all stress from a job, and anyway, some stress can be beneficial. It motivates us to stay on track and get a job completed. Too much, however, can create problems. Take care to watch your stress levels. You can help to manage the stress of your employees only after you have ensured your own well-being.

Here are some ways to manage stress:

1. Realize that stress is something that we create in ourselves. It is an individual reaction to mental or emotional strain. Everyone will have a different stress level and a different reaction to stress. Stress derives from frustration and anxiety coupled with fear. So, the first defense against stress is to understand that it is not the situation but how you respond to it that creates what we experience as stress.

2. Realize that whatever you are facing, it is really not that important. In the big scheme of things, so what? Do not let your mind make more of it than it is.

3. Step back and try to get perspective. Divorce yourself from the situation and look at it from an outsider's point of view. Is the matter at hand worth a heart attack or stroke? Probably not.

4. Take a break and take a walk. Think about things that are really important: your family, your friends, your life. Imagine a beautiful scene in nature. Relax. Meditate. Ask for spiritual guidance, calmness, and insight.

5. Once you have clamed down, carefully and slowly approach the situation. What are things you can change and things you cannot? Focus only on the things you can change. Don't waste time and emotions on the "would have, could have, should have, if only, or why didn't" factors. It is done; let go of that. You can get all hot and bothered about these things, but you are wasting your time. Move on.

6. Make up a list of what you can reasonably expect to do to address the issues that you can change. If there is a time deadline, can you get it changed? If there is information you need, how can you get it? Where can you find help to achieve as many of the objectives as possible?

7. Work on the list of items, one at a time. Check them off. Proceed carefully but as efficiently as possible. If you are not going to make a deadline, then let people know ahead of time. Ask for help. Relax, work hard, but remember that whatever the task or deadline, it is likely to be arbitrary. Do not try and be a hero, shouldering all this "pressure" to prove something.

8. Take time to meditate during your work. It is amazing how inspiration can come from a little time spent thinking about things from a different perspective.

Be conscious of the amount of work you give your employees. Check with them continually to see how they are doing in managing their workload. Do not overload subordinates to the point where they are overwhelmed. When employees feel overly taxed, they begin experiencing burn out. This is when stress levels will rise. This is not good for performance, and it is not good for the long-term welfare of employees or the organization.

This story illustrates a failure to understand the amount of work someone has to perform:

Mary was married to a male chauvinist. They both worked full-time, but he never did anything around the house and certainly not any housework. That, he declared, was women's work. But one evening, Mary arrived home from work to find the children bathed, a load of wash in the washing machine, dinner on the stove, and a beautifully set dining table. She was astonished and asked her husband, Charley, what was going on. He said that he had read an article that suggested working wives would be more romantically inclined if they were not so tired from having to do all the housework and hold down a full-time job. The next day, she couldn't wait to tell her friends at the office. They asked how it worked out. Mary said, "Well, it was a great dinner. Charley even cleaned up, helped the kids with their homework, and folded the laundry." One of her friend's asked, "But what about afterward?" "It didn't work out," Mary said. "Charley was too tired."

Are You Too Stressed?

It is important to recognize stress-related problems early on before you become overloaded. Take measures to deal with it before the problem gets out of hand. Look for these symptoms:

- ✓ You feel tired at work and lack energy.

- ✓ You become easily irritated at work.

- ✓ You feel like everyone is on your case to get things done.

- ✓ You can't seem to get anything done; your productivity is poor, and vital projects get ignored.

- ✓ You can't seem to get started on a project; you procrastinate for no reason.

- ✓ Doing a good job is less of a priority for you than it used to be.

- ✓ You drag your feet all morning or have trouble getting out of bed because the thought of going to work is torturous.

- ✓ Work is becoming increasingly boring, even activities you used to enjoy seem tedious.

- ✓ Your attitude toward your job, company, supervisors or coworkers has become increasingly negative.

- ✓ Work, its consequences, and feelings toward it are affecting your personal life.

- ✓ Your sleeping and eating patterns have changed, either increasing or decreasing markedly.

You need to be aware that being stressed out can be symptomatic of clinical depression. If you exhibit these symptoms, you should seek professional assistance from a psychologist or other mental health professional.

Manage workloads carefully. Be sensitive to people's stress levels by observing them and asking them directly how they are doing. Remember that your goal as a leader is not simply to get them to finish the current project. It is to keep them functioning at a high level for many years. You must also be attentive to your own mental and physical health. To promote long-term health, you must take care of stress on a daily basis.

Chapter Analysis

Keys to Understanding

- A certain level of stress is expected; that's why it's a job.

- Keep tabs on your workers' stress levels and help them with time management as necessary.

- Remember the long-range goals and do not burn people out every time a new project comes up.

Questions for Reflection

1. In what ways can you relieve your own stress levels?

2. How will you effectively gauge your employees' stress levels?

The Little Things

To make sacrifices in big things is easy, but to make sacrifices in little things is what we are seldom capable of.

—Goethe

Kindness can become its own motive. We are made kind by being kind.

—Eric Hoffer

Leaders often overlook the fact that little things mean a great deal to people. I see leaders continually underestimate their impact on people in their organizations. You do not have to slay giant dragons daily as a leader. Sometimes, you just keep paying attention to small matters, and the big things seem to take care of themselves.

Employees need to know that you care. Certainly you can show them this care by doing the big things, but the major issues do not come along very often. Small things come along all day, every single day and provide leaders with great opportunities if they are only perceptive enough to recognize them.

Some examples of some of the "small things" I've done in recent times:

- An employee's wife was sick and had to go to the hospital. I called him afterward to ensure that everything was okay and to offer my assistance if needed.

- One employee was involved in a traffic collision. Although he was not injured, I drove out to the scene to check on him.

- Several of our employees mentioned that although coffee was provided, it would be nice to have some hot chocolate as well. I got them a huge box of hot chocolate.

- One employee failed at a promotional examination he was expected to pass. I sought him out, consoled him, and offered my assistance to review information so that he would have a better chance of passing the next time.

I know that these are not seemingly significant issues, but I can assure you that people remember when you do such things. They really are important to people, and if you are on the lookout for such opportunities, you will find that there will be plenty of them to act on. This is the part of leadership that requires extreme sensitivity to the needs and mood of your workplace. It is an area in which demonstrated loyalty to employees on your part can reap tremendous personal and organizational rewards.

People are not concerned about big, faceless corporations. They are not loyal to companies that show no concern for them. As the leader, you are the representative of your company. You have the ability to shape how employees view their own organization by how you treat them. You have the opportunity, and indeed the responsibility, to create a positive, loyal workforce by using your observation, sensitivity, and empathy to provide employees with a positive work environment.

Chapter Analysis

Keys to Understanding

- Do the little things right; the big things will follow.

- Small efforts combined together can equal large successes.

Questions for Reflection

1. What are the little things that you could do to show that you care about employees?

2. How do you prevent privilege from becoming entitlement?

3. How do the organization's policies show care and concern for employees?

Treat People Unequally

There can never be human happiness in a society that imposes a rule of "equality" which disregards merit and rewards incompetence.

–David Lawrence

It sounds odd to say that you should not treat people equally, so let me explain. Everyone in your organization should receive a minimum baseline of respect and courtesy. This is true even of your most "problem" employee, the one you would most like to rid from your organization. Beyond this though, you do not have to treat everyone equally. My behavior toward employees is directly tied to the effort they extend.

I am sure that there are certain people in your organization who are your "go-to" people. These are the people that do the most work, do the best work, work best under pressure, and never seem to call in sick. For these people, I will do almost anything they ask of me that is within my power.

Why? If they are "busting their humps" for me, then I should be doing the same for them. It may take the form of allowing them a flexible schedule. It may be helping them to accommodate their college requirements. It may be helping them to get that special day off. Whatever it is, I am at their service.

On the other hand, I will not go to the wall for the people that fall below the standard. I will help them within reason, but I will only go above and beyond to the same extent that they do. For uncommitted, mediocre, marginal people, I will accord them the aforementioned baseline of respect and courtesy but not much more.

This type of treatment may be viewed as a type of motivation. The harder you work, the more consideration you will get when you make a special request. I believe that reward should be tied to merit. I am not being partial to people for my own personal reasons but rather for their work records and demonstrated efforts.

For example, if I see an employee who is working extra hours, helping out when needed, and putting in a great deal of effort, I am more apt to work with them when they need a day off. On the other hand, if the person shows up late, slacks off most of the day, and gets little work done, I will not go all out to help this person. My effort is directly related to their performance.

When confronted with a request, I will tell the employee why I am not granting or supporting the request. We will discuss what behaviors would result in my supporting them. This is sometimes an enlightening conversation for the employee. They have a concrete example of the results of their behavior.

What if someone accuses me of treating people differently? I will confess to my approach with no remorse. I think that this is what is best for the organization. I believe it sends a strong, clear message as to the type of employee that is desired. The less committed employees may accuse me of favoritism and inconsistency, but I can live with that.

I would encourage all leaders to take the same approach. Understand though that this is a controversial tactic, and it may not work or be acceptable in every organization. You may want to check organizational policy on individual procedures. Furthermore, you won't necessarily be the most popular person in town, but then leadership is not supposed to be a popularity contest.

Chapter Analysis

Keys to Understanding

- Treat everyone in your organization with a baseline level of respect.

- Treat your best people as if they were worth their weight in gold (because they are).

Questions for Reflection

1. In what ways might you encourage a marginal person to become a star performer?

2. If you show favoritism to a star performer, how does that affect the dynamic of that employee with the other coworkers?

3. How do you correctly identify a star performer?

Firing

Failure is, in a sense, the highway to success, inasmuch as every discovery of what is false leads us to seek earnestly after what is true.

–John Keatts

What is defeat? Nothing but education. Nothing but the first step to something better.

–Wendell Phillips

It might seem odd to find a chapter on firing in a section related to concern for people. However, when forced to take such an action, the ultimate test is to be able to maintain a concern for the person involved. One of the most common misconceptions that employees have about firing is that it is enjoyable to take such actions. Show me a person who thinks it is fun to fire an employee, and I will show you someone who has never had to do it.

I have been involved in many cases that resulted in firing. Some were trainees; some were probationary employees; some were tenured employees who were fired for poor performance; some were tenured employees who were fired for engaging in misconduct. Every single one of these cases was a difficult experience for me. Even if the employee deserved it, the act of firing is painful and awkward. Firing someone is a gut-wrenching action, and it is one of the duties that I least enjoy about leadership.

That being said, sometimes firing has to be done when it is in the best interest of the organization. No one person, no matter how high up, can be allowed to drag everyone else down. Employees are required to carry their own weight and act in accordance with law, policy, and procedure. They are expected to be capable and competent. If not, termination of employment may be the result.

If your position requires that you fire people when necessary, you will be known by such lovely names as "assassin" and "hatchet man." Sometimes, your popularity will decline because of the actions that you had to take. The truth of these situations may be distorted completely by rumor and speculation. It is your job, however, to distance yourself personally from this. You will have responsibilities as a leader that you do not enjoy, but that comes with the territory.

An example of this happened to me once when a popular and tenured employee had to be terminated. There was absolutely no question that this employee needed to be fired; it was not even a close call. As it happened, the case wrapped up almost on Christmas Day. Firing someone at Christmas is not my idea of a good time, whether they deserved it or not. So, the employee was kept on the payroll for two weeks beyond Christmas out of compassion for his family and the time of the year. A week into the new year, he was terminated.

Although this happened many years ago, to this day there is still talk about how poor old so-and-so was fired intentionally on Christmas. As I said, it is not a popularity contest, and sometimes you do not come out unscathed. This can happen even when you make every effort to be fair and compassionate. This is the responsibility of leadership.

There are a few final points on firing someone. First, if you're going to fire someone, you need to look the person in the eye while doing so. You do not e-mail the person; you do not send a memo; you surely do not call in a consultant.

Give the person the respect of a face-to-face meeting. There may be exceptions to this in cases where it is reasonably anticipated that the employee may become violent. I am sensitive to this concern, as being in law enforcement, most of the people I have had to fire came to the meeting with a gun strapped to their hip. However, this concern for security must not be used to mask inadequacy or cowardice of the boss when it is time to fire an individual.

Secondly, if you are positively convinced that someone needs to be fired, do it quickly. I have seen leaders struggle forever with this issue, even when they knew for a fact that the person had to be fired. If you are sure, do not waste time (Christmas Day excluded, of course).

Thirdly, remember that being let go may be one of the best things that can happen to an employee. As old doors are shut, new ones may open for that person. The leader must respect the fact that the employee is not performing as expected and probably is quite unhappy. Also, it is more often the case than not that the employee sees it coming.

Remember that firing can be a therapeutic thing for the employee. Thus, try and frame it as positively as possible. Oftentimes it is helpful to begin the conversation by a brief review of that person's performance, concluding with something along the lines of "it is obvious that you are not happy here."

Try to frame it from the employee's perspective. If one is not happy, not doing well, unable or unwillingly to complete the work, or cannot adhere to company policy, then it is in this person's best interest to be separated from the company. Conclude that it is not worth it for them to be unhappy, and therefore a separation is best. They will then be free to pursue an opportunity that is better suited for them. Express your support and offer to help them (and mean it).

Also remember that for most people getting fired is one of the most traumatic events of their entire lives. Be as gentle and compassionate as you possibly can under the circumstances. Even if you are upset with the person, present the news in a caring manner.

Finally, if you lose sleep over having to fire someone, don't worry. This is normal. I would only tell you to worry if you were able to fire people without losing any sleep. Most likely, this task is going to be stressful and perhaps emotionally disturbing for you. You are human. Do not see this as a weakness.

It is very important that you follow the law and good-business practices before you fire someone. Be sure that you have the grounds for firing documented. Be sure that you have a written record of the events surrounding the firing. Never fire someone on the spot out of anger. When you fire someone, be sure that you have a witness and make a written record of what you said.

It is generally best to have the employee accompanied from that point forward. The person should be entrusted to get all personal belongings and leave the premises immediately. Do not allow an employee who has been terminated to go to lunch with other employees, be alone, or have access to files or computers after the news is delivered. Be sure to have a list of items that they are responsible for returning (such as keys, etc.). Do not issue a final paycheck until such items are returned.

Chapter Analysis

Key to Understanding

- Before firing someone, make sure that you have done everything in your power to help that person succeed.

- If firing is necessary, do not drag the process out for months because you find the task daunting.

- When you do have to fire a person, be as gentle and compassionate as the situation allows.

Questions for Reflection

1. How do you react to the prospect of terminating an employee? Do you see it as positive in some ways for the employee?

2. How can you help an employee in the termination process?

3. Do employees have a clear idea of what constitutes grounds for dismissal?

Final Thoughts

In speeches, General H. Norman Schwarzkopf has said that leaders in the 21st century must have two things: competence and character. I could not agree more. I think that the concepts of *The Call to Lead* will be of great assistance to you in becoming a better leader. The skills discussed in this book combined with the natural talents you can develop through introspection should help you with this process. However, without competence and character, you will not have much of a leadership foundation on which to build. Take a hard look at yourself in the mirror and search for answers to your competence and character. If you are lacking in either, you have a great deal of contemplation ahead of you before you are ready to be a good leader.

Two very difficult things to handle in life are success and failure. As a leader, even a good one, you will have many instances of both. The important thing is how you choose to respond. Make no mistake, it is in fact a choice on your part. Perhaps leadership has been thrust upon you within your organization, and you are concerned that you are not up for the task. It will take hard work, but this may be your time to rise to the occasion.

Sometimes, you will have difficult decisions to make. Choose the course of action that benefits people the most. When two courses benefit people equally, choose the boldest course of action – it is more fun. When you shoot for the moon, even if you miss, you'll still be among the stars. Take the time to evaluate and develop your own intuition, empathy, and sense of timing. Be passionate about your role as a leader. You have more impact and influence than you will ever know.

Listen to your inner voice and do not be afraid to "make waves" if you truly believe in the cause. You must develop a spiritual centeredness where you know what you believe in and are willing to stand up for it. You should not compromise your morals to please someone else, even if this person is your boss. Develop your own sense of moral courage. You may want to practice situational leadership but never practice situational ethics. Take the time to meditate on what it means to be a good leader and then evaluate yourself within this context.

Finally, remember the old saying that goes: on their deathbed, no one has ever said that they wished they had spent more time at the office. Work hard but be balanced in life. With a healthy balance in your life, you'll be able to be a more balanced leader. In the end, leadership is a challenge and a reward. Being a leader means applying the Golden Rule within the context of an organization or business arena. Your reward will be your own growth as an individual and the chance to change people's lives by helping them to grow and fulfill their destinies.

Appendix:

Organizational Evaluation for Employees

Use this survey to gain feedback from your employees or from a specific focus group. It will give you insight as to where organizational strengths are and what factors need improvement. It will also help you to evaluate your own leadership style.

1. What do you believe to be the top goals of the organization?

2. How clear are the organization's vision and its policies?

   - ❏ Very clear
   - ❏ Fairly clear
   - ❏ Not very clear
   - ❏ Not clear at all

3. Do you witness any conflict between the organization's goals and/or vision and its policies?

   - ❏ Yes, a lot of conflict
   - ❏ Yes, some conflict
   - ❏ Yes, a little conflict
   - ❏ No conflict

4. How clear are your boss's expectations for you and goals for your performance?

    ❑ Very clear
    ❑ Somewhat clear
    ❑ Not very clear
    ❑ Not clear at all

5. Do you think that objectives and goals are widely understood throughout the organization?

    ❑ A lot of understanding
    ❑ Some understanding
    ❑ Very little understanding
    ❑ No understanding

6. Do you see your boss as a mentor, someone you can turn to if you need help or have a problem?

    ❑ Very approachable and helpful
    ❑ Somewhat approachable and helpful
    ❑ Not very helpful, a little distant
    ❑ Not at all helpful, difficult to approach

7. In what ways do you feel that your boss supports you?

8. Are there areas in which you need more support than you are currently receiving?

9. How much do you feel that coworkers support one another?

    ❑ A great deal of support
    ❑ Good amount or average support
    ❑ Very little support
    ❑ No support

10. Do you believe that there are positive working relationships in the organization?

    ❑ Very positive relationships
    ❑ Somewhat positive relationships
    ❑ Somewhat negative relationships
    ❑ Very negative relationships

11. How much teamwork takes place within the organization?

    ❑ A great deal
    ❑ Some, an average amount
    ❑ Little teamwork
    ❑ No teamwork

12. How responsible are you for managing your work and creating your own systems and methods to handle tasks?

    ❑ Very responsible
    ❑ Somewhat responsible
    ❑ A little responsible
    ❑ Not at all responsible

13. How does the way in which your boss or the organization structure tasks impact your ability to perform at your best?

        ❑ Affected to a great extent quite often
        ❑ Affected somewhat occasionally
        ❑ Affected minimally and not very often
        ❑ Not affected at all

14. Is there a strong emphasis put on recognizing problems and resolving conflict?

        ❑ A great deal of emphasis
        ❑ Some emphasis
        ❑ Little emphasis
        ❑ No emphasis

15. On a normal, daily basis, how smoothly do operations run in the organization?

        ❑ Very smoothly
        ❑ Pretty smoothly
        ❑ Somewhat smoothly
        ❑ Not very smoothly

16. How well does your boss keep everything running?

        ❑ Very well
        ❑ Fairly well
        ❑ Somewhat poorly
        ❑ Very poorly

17. Are you regularly recognized and rewarded when you do a good job?

  ❑ Very often
  ❑ Fairly frequently
  ❑ Very rarely
  ❑ Never

18. Are the rewards motivating you?

  ❑ Very much
  ❑ Somewhat
  ❑ Not really
  ❑ Not at all

19. Is your performance regularly evaluated?

  ❑ Very frequently
  ❑ Somewhat frequently
  ❑ Very rarely
  ❑ Not at all

20. Is the criticism that you receive constructive and helpful?

  ❑ Very
  ❑ Somewhat
  ❑ Not really
  ❑ Not at all

21. In what specific ways has your boss worked individually with you to help you develop and improve?

22. Do your boss's actions demonstrate good teamwork?

   ❑ Very much
   ❑ Somewhat
   ❑ Not really
   ❑ Not at all

23. Is your boss open to employee suggestions regarding the workplace, tasks, or improvements?

   ❑ Very open
   ❑ Somewhat open
   ❑ Not very open
   ❑ Not open

24. Are people treated fairly and equally with basic respect and concern?

   ❑ Very fair and equal treatment
   ❑ Mainly fair and equal treatment
   ❑ Some unfair and unequal treatment
   ❑ Great deal of unfair and unequal treatment

25. What is the organization's and the boss's reaction to failure and mistakes? Are people held accountable for their own mistakes? Are they still supported after messing up?

26. Do you believe that you received adequate training to perform your job well?

   ❑ Yes
   ❑ No

27. Do you feel that you are receiving adequate ongoing training, educational opportunities, and/or resources to continue to perform well?

       ❑ Yes
       ❑ No

28. Are changes in the organization well communicated, well explained, and well planned?

       ❑ All the time
       ❑ Usually
       ❑ Sometimes
       ❑ Rarely
       ❑ Never

29. Do you feel that good communication occurs in the organization? Are you kept informed about what is happening? Do you feel that your voice is heard when you have ideas or concerns?

Additional Comments:

References

Bennis, Warren G. <u>Managing People is Like Herding Cats</u>.
Cambridge: Perseus Pub., 2000.

Blanchard, Kenneth H. and Spencer Johnson. <u>The One
Minute Manager</u>. La Jolla, CA: Blanchard-Johnson
Publishers, 1982.

Childress, John R. and Larry E. Senn. <u>The Secret of a Winning
Culture: Building High-Performance Teams</u>. Los
Angeles: Leadership Press, 1999.

Covey, Stephen R. <u>Principle-Centered Leadership</u>. New York:
Summit Books, 1991.

Hersey, Paul and Kenneth H. Blanchard. <u>Management of
Organizational Behavior: Utilizing Human Resources</u>.
Englewood Cliffs, NJ: Prentice-Hall, 1982.

Kouzes, James M. and Barry Z. Posner. <u>The Leadership
Challenge: How to Get Extraordinary Things Done in
Organizations</u>. San Francisco: Jossey-Bass, 1987.

Loynes, Chris. "Expedition Leadership." <u>Planners Handbook
and Directory 1993-1994</u>. London, Eng.: Expedition
Advisory Centre, Royal Geographical Society.

Phillips, Donald T. <u>Lincoln on Leadership: Executive Strategies
for Tough Times</u>. New York: Warner Books, 1992.

Sashkin, Marshall and Kenneth J. Kiser. <u>Putting Total Quality Management to Work: What TQM Means, How to Use It, and How to Sustain It over the Long Run</u>. San Francisco: Berrett-Koehler, 1993.

Tannenbaum, Robert and Warren H. Schmidt. "How to Choose a Leadership Pattern." *Harvard Business Review*. Boston: Harvard Business School, March/April 1958.

Townsend, Robert. <u>Further Up the Organization</u>. New York: Knopf, 1984.

Van Oech, Roger. <u>A Whack on the Side of the Head: How to Unlock Your Mind for Innovation</u>. Menlo Park, CA: Creative Think, 1983.